SUPER HERPES

A NERD's harrowing story
of DATING, DEBAUCHERY,
and DISILLUSIONMENT in Silicon Valley

COLIN BUNDSCHU

"There's no shortcut to a dream. It's all blood and sweat, and life is what you manage in between."

—JAMES MERCER

Start Here

WANT YOU TO IMAGINE for a moment that you are a man in your mid-twenties, sitting on a bed. Not just any bed, mind you: this is *your* bed. It's very late, a little shy of two o'clock in the morning on a Saturday night, and you're sober and tired. In your hands, you hold four cards with varying illustrations of gemstones and luxury goods. Immediately in front of you are the remaining cards and pieces of the board game Jaipur (never mind if you don't know what that game is—just imagine Monopoly). Just across from you is someone you have known for a few years, a girl your age who holds four cards of her own. She is wire-thin and has long, straight blond hair. Her angular face sports soft green eyes. You two are alone and facing each other, and although this is not a strip game or foreplay, you are both completely naked. As such, the two of you are awkwardly avoiding eye contact, and you both stare intently at the cards you hold while trying to figure out how exactly you ended up in this situation.

Hold on to that thought for a moment while we take a step back.

You might be wondering what the heck you are holding right now—a book called *Super Herpes* is certain to raise some eyebrows (personally I prefer just one, but it's your face). A brief explanation is that this is a memoir of my romantic misadventures as a software engineer and video game designer living in Silicon Valley. Yet despite the expectation of wisdom and experience that comes with a word like "memoir," I am, as of writing, only twenty-six years old. This makes me (somewhat necessarily) inexperienced at life and, likely, also a bit unwise. What could a young man like myself have to offer in the way of a memoir about my romantic experiences?

Before I answer this, I want to give a quick overview of what exactly Silicon Valley is. Geographically, it's an area in California that starts roughly at the southern half of the San Francisco Peninsula and ends at about San Jose. This marks out an approximately rectangular suburban/office park region of about thirty miles by ten miles, a substantial fraction of the larger San Francisco Bay Area. The area is home to the headquarters of some of the largest software companies in the world, including Google, Facebook, Apple, and Oracle, to name just a few. It's chock-full of software engineers and "techies," and the inspiration for the spookily accurate show of the same name. (For those wondering, the area is not named Silicon Valley because this is where silicon is mined—it's because silicon is an essential component in semiconductors, the secret sauce of a computer, and there are a lot of computer companies here. I was very confused by this at first!)

For most, the prospect of spending a life tediously winding and unwinding complex computer programs is highly unappealing. Consequently, software engineering, and resultantly Silicon Valley, attracts somewhat peculiar people who think in a highly structured and analytical manner, a trend to which I am no exception. This peculiarity often makes software engineers difficult to interact with, as they have a hard time turning off that highly critical part of their brain when engaging in social activities. To our credit, this tends to make us open and forward about our thoughts, although in much the same way as a wildly swung sledgehammer is open and forward about bruising flesh and breaking bones. But even more so, this type of thinking tends to manifest itself in the form of borderline-obsessive hobbies and colossal personal projects, such as giant basement railroad sets and arena-combat robots.

In my case, I took that energy and applied it to the most pressing problem I saw before me: the search for that special someone to spend the rest of my life with. Through careful optimization and diligent study, I tried to solve romance in the same way I would debug a broken computer program. The resulting quest, which dominated a year and a half of my life, took me on an astonishing 84 first dates and another 35 or so second dates, with the grand total of all dates approaching around 150 in that span. It goes without saying that this cadence is atypical, as this is more first dates than most people will go on in their entire lives.

In addition to being notable for its sheer volume, this quest had a few more "exciting" twists and turns beyond the mundane repetition you might expect from so many random meetups. "Exciting" is certainly an apt word to be using here, because my romantic encounters encompass getting into high-speed car accidents, being erotically choked in a bar, dodging the advances of corporate vice presidents, engaging in clandestine romance, and of course, playing a naked game of Jaipur. I might even say that the aggregate of this experience has been insanely terrifying—except for the undeniable fact that at times it has been quite enjoyable as well!

But as I looked back on the chaotic events that transpired, I began to wonder why this adventure turned out as bizarrely as it did. Naturally, I turned to the only person I knew who could give it to me straight: Joseph.

Joseph is, beyond a doubt, the most inoffensive human I have ever had the pleasure of meeting. I don't just mean this in terms of looks—although his six feet of height, mysteriously tan ethnicity, slightly wavy black hair, and disarming smile give him a rather pleasing visual quality. Instead, his likability comes from his calm and measured voice, which gives him a welcoming and nonjudgmental demeanor. This is somewhat remarkable, given the fact that he is a programmer, like me, and thus should be predisposed to honestly objectifying other humans in a manner that is as impersonal as it is abrasive. But by some eldritch magic, Joseph has all of the honesty and none of the abrasiveness. (By some lesser magic, I have all the abrasiveness and none of the honesty. I like to describe this as "rugged charm.")

In early 2016, Joseph and I worked on the same team at the Oculus Virtual Reality division of Facebook. On one afternoon in a spotless and well-stocked kitchen at Facebook's campus in the heart of Silicon Valley, Joseph and I were making some espresso (yes, they have espresso machines at Facebook, along with lots of other stuff I'll tell you about later). I turned to Joseph, who was preparing to steam some milk, and popped the question:

"Joseph, I don't get it. Why does this keep happening to me? Why do I have so many crazy dates?"

Now, in asking this, I was genuinely concerned for my well-being. I had just been mildly strangled on a recent date-gone-awry, and I was beginning to wonder if I had somehow brought this upon myself. After all, I could no longer keep count of my dates simply by taking off my shoes, and the lack of success was beginning to give me pause for thought.

As I asked this, Joseph was standing in front of the espresso machine, and he weighed my words as he pulled a lever that sent a rush of heated water vapor into his lactation-filled cup.

"Colin, did you ever see the movie *Yes Man* with Jim Carrey?"

I watched the milk begin to swirl and froth in the cup in front of him. "Yes."

Joseph drove the steaming wand deeper into the milk, creating a small whirlpool. His eyes remained focused on the task, but his calm smile showed his continued attention to our conversation. "Remember how he said yes to things literally anyone else would have said no to, and then hilarity and sometimes misfortune ensued?" Joseph glanced up for a moment, giving me one of his characteristically warm looks.

I looked back at him, narrowing my eyes in confusion and frowning ever so slightly. "Yeah?"

Joseph turned off the machine and removed the wand. He looked at me fully now, his face showing mild amusement. "*That* is your dating life." He smacked the metal heating cup on the counter and swirled it around before combining it with his espresso shot.

Effectively, Joseph was saying that my light-speed dating quest had been what happens when you check "D, all the above" on the list of questionable opportunities available to you in life and combine it with a relentless drive to keep dating, despite the mind-bogglingly bad consequences that began to pile up.

So, let's try tackling that first question again: What are you holding right now?

Well, this is the story of what happens when a highly motivated and obsessive software engineer sits down and attacks the search for love like a coding problem: by throwing a lot of time, energy, and critical thinking at it until *something* breaks. This is the story of the absolute insanity that ensued. And most important, this is a story about a game of Jaipur.

A Portrait of the Author
as a Young Nerd

T O TRULY APPRECIATE both the vigor and insanity with which I went about my dating crusade, we must go back to an earlier time—to the mystical land of the 1990s. My story begins in a boring suburban town in western Washington State by the name of Silver Firs. As a distant satellite of Seattle, this town is remarkable in no particular aspect, save for the fact that it used to have a buffalo farm nearby, which has now been replaced by strip malls. From this canonical American backdrop, I grew up as the annoying and inquisitive kind of brat that drives both adults and fellow children absolutely nuts.

The reason? I was that kid who would never stop talking. Ever.

I don't know what it was about me—maybe I just enjoyed the melodious (read as: nasally) timbre of my own voice—but by age five, I would brain-dump on anyone who would listen. At my father's company Christmas parties, I would bend the ears of coworkers and fake Santas alike, regaling them with arcane facts I had dug up in encyclopedias and through Netscape. Ever wonder what the chief export of Bolivia is? No? Well, I don't care; I'm telling you anyway. (It's petroleum, for those who are wondering.)

The combination of being unusually well read and quite verbose about it gave me the reputation of a know-it-all and, unfortunately, also correlated with a lot of difficulty in making friends. I think this backdrop is a familiar one to most engineers, who largely grow up far too convinced they know everything about the world to be remotely tolerable when they open their mouths. However, this placed me in a fantastic position to succeed in school, and I received high grades for my entire academic life. Yet, despite my stellar scholastic performance on paper, the clear majority of my time *in* school was spent earning the ire of my teachers. I achieved this through varied means, including playing video games, talking with friends, sleeping, or a combination thereof. I can't remember a time when my classroom behavior was anything better than "unsatisfactory."

But even though I didn't gel with classroom etiquette, attending class gave me my first introduction to the world of romance. This happened in kindergarten, where I met this girl, Rachel. Using all my charm and wit, I picked a dandelion from the grass in front of school and gave it to her. She said it was pretty, and I said *she* was pretty. One day we kissed behind the tire swing in the playground. However, as soon as our lips touched, I knew I had done something wrong. Racked with guilt, I ran crying to the teacher and told her exactly what had happened. It never worked out with Rachel.

When I wasn't trying to woo the other kindergartners, I spent most of my time biking around the more rural parts of Washington with my two-years-younger brother, Christian. We spent many an afternoon catching snakes, poking dead opossums with sticks, making forts under upturned-tree roots, and generally exploring the uninhabited areas near my house. However, this changed once we began to realize the entertainment potential of the computer in our house, which happened around the time I reached middle school. Of course, we had both been introduced to the computer much earlier than that (there is a great family photo of six-year-old Colin playing the computer game Diablo on my father's lap), but it wasn't until now that computers could keep up with the excitement potential of dead opossums in the woods.

Unfortunately, computers were still rather expensive in the early 2000s, and this meant that our family had just one. Thus, my brother and I fought constantly over who got to use it. Honestly, I don't know that we did much other than play video games or punch one another from the time this transition occurred. This bitter contest over the precious computer resource became the defining factor in our relationship and, as the years passed, it would transform our previous coexistence as exploration buddies into one of contentious rivals.

But around this same time, my romantic endeavors became more pronounced. Video games and fistfights had taught me to be both persistent and brave, and I carried these traits over to my attempts at dating. If I was interested in a girl, I didn't just pick a flower and hand it to her: I asked her out.

Unfortunately, as a middle-schooler, I was still a nasal know-it-all. Except now I had the additional benefit of glasses and a dollop of bowl-cut Bieber brown hair. (Quite the stud, no?) Thus, my forward attitude toward dating didn't work so well. I got a lot of rejections.

But I was undeterred. Much like how a failed boss fight in Diablo would spur me to try harder next time, these dating failures only tempered my resolve. My whole life was ahead of me, and if I was going to be a Supreme Court justice, an astronaut, *and* a video game designer, then I needed to get a head start on this family thing. I wish I could say that I was joking, but that was literally my rationale.

By my junior year in high school, I had unsuccessfully asked out exactly twenty girls. For some reason, I was rather proud of this fact, as it signified a certain level of commitment. But at this point my antics were public knowledge, and that fact was certainly not doing me any favors. Yet just after Christmas of my junior year, I finally succeeded in getting my first girlfriend. The lucky lady was a tall, brunette girl by the name of Ilene who played the drums for the school band and, like me, wore glasses.

Now, I couldn't play drums to save my life, let alone anything else that would have been remotely acceptable for band. But despite this fact, much of my social interaction involved hanging out with friends in the band room. Ilene, who was one of the people in our group, slowly developed a friendship with me over several months. One night, I mustered the courage to ask her to play the board game Risk, and it was over that game that we shared a fateful kiss. (For the life of me I can't imagine why I thought Risk was a good date idea, but I guess it worked out.)

The day after our board game, we jointly decided that we would be boyfriend and girlfriend. And although we did not have any opportunities for romance over the coming week, it was not long before we were out of school for one of the rare snowstorms that hit Seattle from time to time.

With the windfall, I'd decided to hop into my purple minivan the evening after the storm and drive the half-mile to her house. (Having had zero experience driving in snow, I "bumped" into two trees along the way.) When I arrived, she bundled up in a fuzzy purple jacket, and we went walking in a meadow turned wintery wonderland. We came to a bench and stopped, just beneath a streetlight.

The yellowy light shone down through flurries of powder, creating slowly changing patterns all around us. We leaned in for a kiss, as delicately as the softly falling snow speckled our winter coats. When we pulled back, we looked deep into each other's eyes, and she said:

"If you ever break up with me, I will burn everything that reminds me of you."

The next day, I broke it off. (I mean come on! That's just crazy.)

Fortunately, I was spared her cleansing fire, and a couple of short years later I found new freedom as a student at Harvey Mudd College, a small school of just eight hundred students located on the eastern edge of Los Angeles County.

While at Harvey Mudd, I studied Computer Science. And even though I enjoyed my major a lot more than my previous schooling, I still couldn't behave properly in class. But now, I could put my learnings to use to avoid it entirely. For example, I wrote an "alarm clock" computer program where if I clicked the "snooze" button when I woke in the morning, it would email one of thirty preloaded excuses to all the professors whose classes I had before noon. It could even automatically download my calendar from Google. The program worked fantastically, up until I let slip that I had been using it at a Computer Science faculty dinner (pro tip: don't do that).

Dating-wise, I had a bit more luck than in high school, which resulted in two girlfriends and a mere twenty-five days spent as a single man in the four years I was at the university. Additionally, I had lost none of the earnest drive that I'd previously taken toward dating, as I was still serious about having kids and raising a family someday. My thinking was that even if these relationships didn't work out, the skills I learned from them would be invaluable for the remainder of my romantic life. After all, if I wanted to be a good husband, wouldn't I have to learn how to be a good boyfriend first?

Of course, there is a huge difference between the intentions you bring into a relationship and how things go. And indeed, for my college romances, good intentions did not prevent these relationships from turning into turbulent affairs.

Regarding my first college girlfriend, I had the delight of introducing her to my best friend during a night of Mario Kart and drinking in my dorm lounge. It was one of those magic moments where two people's eyes meet, and in them you can see not just a spark, but a blazing fire. The kind of fire that connects two kindred spirits in the way that only happens in movies. This was a rather unfortunate turn for me, though, because the thing I saw burning in my girlfriend's eyes was our relationship. And not only would this vision-in-the-flames prove accurate, but the ensuing breakup ended up sending me to the ER when I had my head smashed into a brick wall by her twin sister! Hard to know where the line between daytime television and real life ends sometimes, right? No? It's just me? Crap.

In any case, my second girlfriend and I had a slightly better time of it. Her name was Stella, and we met through our shared class, Principles of Computer Science, where we were required to rotate through partners. Stella was one year above me, and a short, black-haired chemistry major from the adjoining college of Pomona, who was taking computer science classes to bolster her coding skills. She was in fantastic shape from being an avid runner, and her long hair reflected this fact, as it was much lighter at the tips from all the sun. Our fates became intertwined when we became coding partners after I'd discovered she'd been the only one to beat me on the midterm, and I was impressed (read as: jealous).

We spent a few weeks working on class assignments together, and the two of us hit it off. Late nights of coding homework interspersed with the occasional game of Boggle slowly morphed into multi-hour crossword sessions interspersed with Taco Bell. And as fate would have it, we both found ourselves single before too long. This fact was not lost on me when just a few days later, as the two of us shared pizza bagels and debated whether Archaic Scottish words were Scrabble-legal, I got a feeling that this girl was something special. That maybe I wouldn't ever want to stop debating the finer points of Scrabble ruling with her. I wasted no time in asking her out, and much to my delight, the answer was an enthusiastic yes.

For the next year and a half, Stella and I made a pretty bang-up couple. We both loved to go to Jack in the Box at 3:00 a.m. just about every night of the week, and when we weren't playing word games we usually whittled the time away with Pokémon (not Pokémon GO, I mean the *real* game made for Nintendo handhelds). During the winters, we would take snowboarding trips to the mountains near Los Angeles, which by some weird phenomenon had not one but three reasonably good ski resorts.

However, our relationship was not without its faults. We tended to get into spats quite frequently, which was not entirely surprising considering we were both highly contentious intellectuals. Our strong, confident natures often meant that we butted heads on even the smallest of issues, something which kept a perennial low level of strain hanging over our heads.

This strain started to amplify when, at the beginning of my senior year, Stella began attending a PhD chemistry program at Stanford, four hundred miles away in the heart of Silicon Valley. The long distance only added to the challenges of our relationship, an effect that grew as I neared graduation. For, despite being a Computer Science major and having ample job prospects in Silicon Valley, I had accepted an offer to work at Microsoft Game Studios in Seattle, a once-in-a-lifetime opportunity to break into the notoriously difficult to enter video game industry. For me, it was a dream come true. And as I sold it to Stella, after a few years of branding my résumé with Microsoft's sterling name, I could move down to Silicon Valley and the two of us could reunite.

But moving to a state without my girlfriend—and with just a few college friends—left a social void, and to fill it I reconnected with people I'd known in high school. My relationship with Stella became a secondary concern as I struggled to reestablish my roots. Similarly, Stella was developing her own social network at Stanford, and as that first post-collegiate year passed, things began to look grim for the two of us. We had now been in a long-distance relationship for two years, and there was no end in sight. We both stopped putting in the energy necessary to maintain our connection and our relationship began to crumble.

Things finally reached a breaking point in the summer of 2014 after a particularly acrimonious trip to London together. The whole time we argued over where we would eat and which attractions were worthy of our time. After we traveled home to our respective states, miserable and burnt out from a vacation turned sour, another cloud developed over the situation. I had been a Microsoft software engineer for almost a year and a half, and I was now looking to move up in the industry and find a job as a game designer. However, upon checking my email when getting back to the States, I discovered that all my applications in Silicon Valley had been rejected. I called Stella up: I couldn't get a job in her town and I was sick of long distance. It was over.

If this makes the breakup sound rather stoic and cold, I want to emphasize that it wasn't. Even though I was the one who officially ended it, I was in tears during the whole call (even just writing this made me tear up a little). But the deed had been done, and I was officially a free man, able to pursue my creative ambitions. In a short month, I landed a sick job as a midlevel designer at Rockstar Games in San Diego, the company responsible for such monumental titles as Grand Theft Auto, Max Payne, and Red Dead Redemption. I was officially on my way to living the dream.

The Promised Land

BEFORE WE DIVE INTO the sunshiny world of San Diego, there were about two months of time where I was single and still living in Seattle. If there is an official turning point in my life, the point where things officially go from pretty darn good to substantially worse, these two months were it. This is where our story begins.

Seattle, being my hometown and place of adult residence for a year and a half, is a city with which I am intimately familiar. And if I had to summarize it using a single mood, I would choose that frustrating feeling of being hungry yet nothing sounding good to eat. This is because the dominant feature of the city—the weather— is constantly in a state of not knowing what the heck it is doing, yet always wanting to do something else. Usually this results in the weather puttering around between overcast and drizzle, with occasional sudden breaks for sun or rain.

However, working for Microsoft could not have been more the opposite. For those who have seen the show *Silicon Valley*, you might imagine that it involves high pay, great benefits, flexible hours, and tons of perks in the office (like nap pods and gourmet food). Your imagination is spot on—working for Microsoft is exactly like that. I was fortunate to work on their West Campus, which meant that I was within walking distance of a two-story food court, a professional-grade soccer field, and as much free soda and coffee as I could pour down my throat. The food itself wasn't free, but it was discounted. You could get a sushi lunch for ten dollars or an all-you-can-eat Indian buffet for eight dollars (to date, that is still the best butter chicken I have ever had). Inside the food court there was also a bike shop, a salon, an optometrist, a bank, and four major cell phone carrier stores, all of which offered plans discounted below market rate. As lavish as this sounds, by Silicon Valley standards this is modest, if for no other reason than the food wasn't free, and I never once saw a nap pod.

The culture of the company, I would say, was representative of my experiences in software more broadly. My division was heavily male-dominated, like the engineering parts of every software company, and the result was something of a nerd-bro culture. The guys I worked with tended to be introverted, and when they talked (read as: argued) it was about code, video games, or industry current events (like net neutrality). Beyond these stereotypical topics, we also tended to share interests in oddly specific areas, such as aviation. In fact, I knew several pilots at both Microsoft and Facebook, myself included. For the few women in engineering, this type of male-dominant culture was not ideal, but I'll get more into that later.

As for the work, it was a pretty typical office job. I showed up, sat at my computer from eight to ten hours a day to write code, went to a couple of meetings, and then went home. Since I worked in the game division, I trended toward ten to twelve hours a day, and since I was salaried, I didn't see another dime for it. That said, making six figures straight out of college meant that I was hardly complaining.

Given that I was being exceedingly well paid for making video games, those long hours might seem like not such a big deal. I mean, that sounds like a blast, right? That's certainly what I was thinking when I took the job! But this is where the distinction of my role as a software engineer, not a game designer, becomes important. See, as an engineer, it's your job to make the game run, *not* make sure the game is fun or come up with the content. Furthermore, it turns out that writing game code is nearly identical to writing code for any other piece of software, like a personal finance tracker or a pizza delivery app. Sure, you often get to *test* your code by running the game, but I would hardly say that spending a day trying to figure out why the damage on "Thunderfury, Blessed Blade of the Windseeker" isn't reading properly from a configuration file is the fun part of video games. (An astute observer will note that this item is from World of Warcraft, which is *not* a game that I worked on.) It was for this reason that I decided to leave Microsoft to pursue a career as a game designer at Rockstar in San Diego; I wanted to do the fun part, which is designing the game.

In any case, my time living in Seattle and working at Microsoft marked my first foray into dating in the world of tech. And while Seattle is not Silicon Valley in a literal sense, it is in almost all other senses the same experience. The two share a remarkable number of similarities in terms of demographics, culture, and industry, so please pardon me if I use them interchangeably, as I feel this book would not be complete otherwise.

Initially, when I first decided to start dating after finding myself a newly single man in the city of Seattle, I was excited. An entire world of dating apps and options lay before me that hadn't even existed when I was a college student—how amazing would this be? I immediately downloaded and installed Tinder, and before I knew it I was immersed in a flood of single women. Having never used this app before, I had no idea what to expect. I was a lad freshly conscripted into the navy, starry-eyed and bushy-tailed and ready to serve my country at sea. Never mind that I had never seen the ocean before, let alone been on a boat! Compared to the grizzled, salty sailor that is the man I am today, I was filled with as much optimism as I was with stupidity.

When I started, I thought Tinder would be simple. I would throw up a few photos, browse some ladies, see someone I liked, swipe right, and if she liked me we would chat for a bit and then set up a date. I expected that most people maybe spent five or ten minutes a day on it, just casually browsing, and that if I sank in around three hours a night, in a few weeks I could be the king of this whole adult dating scene before I even set foot on the sandy beaches of San Diego to work for Rockstar. After all, this strategy of grinding out success had paid off in both school and work, so why wouldn't it now?

So, that's what I did—I spent three hours a night on Tinder. Well, except that it was closer to five hours a night on weeknights and eight on weekends. Despite the unreasonable time I was putting in, I still expected that it might be a bit rough at first as I learned the ropes. Fortunately, the Internet was absolutely packed with guides, so at least I wasn't fumbling in the dark. My life became very simple: if I wasn't on Tinder, I was reading about it, and if I wasn't doing that I was discussing dating strategies with my coworkers. I was a machine. And after putting in a full two weeks of effort, I sat back and waited for my schedule to fill up.

But as the days passed, for all my effort, I only ended up with one date on the books. I had gone through hundreds—maybe even thousands—of people, and I was striking out left and right (or just left if we want to be technical about it). Even the one girl I had lined up was not that enthused. A graduate student in Tacoma named Amber, she seemed totally put off by the fact that I lived thirty minutes north of her in downtown Seattle. She was basically ready to call it quits right then and there. Having been unable to convince any other girls to go on a date with me since I'd started this whole swiping business, I was persistent. Certain that she was being shortsighted and would be delighted upon meeting me, I offered that we could meet up as conveniently close to her as she wanted. Eventually, she proposed a date at O'Malley's Irish Pub in Tacoma.

Despite the wrangling it had taken, from her photos at least Amber seemed like a real catch. She was slender and tall with straight blond hair that whooshed behind her in dramatic, oceanside photographs. Her delicate features, clear complexion, sharp chin, and athletic body complemented a mysterious smile. Given her comeliness, plus the fact that I had been out of the dating scene for nigh unto four years and was relieved my hours of swiping hadn't been a total waste, I was, to say the least, eager for the date.

The day of the date arrived, and when I rolled up to the bar, I wasn't immediately impressed by her choice in locale. Comparing it in my mind to the upscale (and expensive!) venues and clubs of Belltown, my home district of Seattle, I was made somewhat uneasy by the slew of pickup trucks haphazardly parked on the lawn near the bar. The area was sort of run-down, and the air smelled weird. Yet despite the surroundings, when I stepped inside the old brick building that the pub resided in, the warm wood décor and lively atmosphere immediately put me at ease. On the left was a well-populated seating area with oaken tables and pine chairs, positively buzzing with jovial nighttime activity. In front of me stretched a large wooden bar, as quintessential as the one on the show *Cheers*.

Over my left shoulder I heard a feminine voice: "Colin?"

I turned around to see a short, squat lady about my age addressing me (for clarity, I was twenty-three at the time). Her hair was straight and blond, but her face was not sharp and angular, nor was her complexion clear. Additionally, there was something about her that seemed a bit off. Maybe it was that her odd, quasi-smiling expression made her face look kind of scrunched up.

I paused for a moment. How did this person know my name? After a few seconds of awkwardly staring, I finally figured it out. "Amber?"

The girl before me nodded and motioned toward a couple of stools at the bar. We walked over and sat down. I was alarmed at how different she was from the photos, and my tongue was wrapped up while I tried to digest this. It was as if the photos had been carefully crafted to hide every flaw and to accentuate every positive quality beyond recognition. Fortunately, I had enough class not to pull out my phone for a side-by-side comparison.

As I sat there puzzling, an enormous, bald, bearded man behind the counter turned around. Not missing a beat on the stereotypical bartender look, he was wiping down an old-timey mug with a rag. His voice was deep and rich. "What can I get for you two?"

"I'll have a Guinness," I replied, looking up at the behemoth before me. He nodded and turned toward Amber.

Amber swiveled a bit in her seat, glancing down at the menu. "Yeah, that sounds good. I'll have one as well."

The bartender nodded once more and started to fill a couple of glasses. Instinctively I reached for my wallet. "I got this," I noted. Amber acknowledged with a humph, still staring down at the menu before her.

By now I had come to terms with the fact that this girl must, in fact, be Amber, and I tried to start up a conversation. After all, I had come this far, so I might as well see it through. Unfortunately, I hadn't thought ahead about how one would talk to someone in a setting like this. So without a better plan, I just started asking random questions about her life. It felt more than a bit forced, but things took a more natural turn when I asked her what I thought was an innocuous question:

"So Amber," I started, taking a long swig out of my Guinness while I nervously played with the corner of my menu. I quickly looked up to make sure I made eye contact. The Internet dating guides had said that was very important. "What do you want to do with your life after grad school?" (By the way, this is *exactly* the wrong question to ask a grad student on a date, but a great one if you want to stress them out.)

Despite my venturing into dangerous waters, her response was cool. Nothing on her face showed a hint of discomfort. "Well, I'm going to be the first female president of the United States."

My eyebrows shot up as I looked at her quizzically. I tried to parse the mismatch between her bold statement and her nonchalant demeanor. Her voice was totally deadpan and gave no hint of joking. "Wait, didn't an article come out a couple of months ago in *Time* magazine about how Hillary Clinton is basically unstoppable? [This was late 2014] How are you going to be first if she is going to be first? Do you think she is going to lose?"

Amber shook her head and continued looking at me in a totally normal manner, as if we were discussing something as banal as the weather. The hint of a smile was in the corner of her mouth, and she said with confidence, "I'm just going to be first."

I leaned back and rubbed my neck nervously. "Okay, so how old are you?"

She looked down at her beer, not visibly offended by the question. "Twenty-three."

My expression quickly transformed into one of disbelief and confusion, but I pressed onward. "And you know that you have to be like ... thirty-five? Something like that? To run for president? And they are saying Hillary is likely to win the next election after Obama finishes his second term. How can you be so confident not only that she will lose but that you will even make it so far as to be a contender?"

Amber didn't reply, just returned to sipping on her beer. I continued looking at her intently, still trying to figure out if she was joking, even as her tone suggested that she was not.

Guessing that I was pushing too hard on a joke that didn't land, I changed the topic. "So, I was reading this thing on a dating blog about how the most telling question for a relationship is 'Wouldn't it be fun to chuck it all and go live on a sailboat?' Kind of crazy, huh?"

Amber's expressionless face turned from her beer to me. "Would you?"

I blinked. "Would I what?"

She squared her shoulders as she turned in my direction, looking me dead in the eye. She was neither smiling nor frowning. "Would you chuck it all and go live on a sailboat?"

I laughed nervously, looking down at the bent-up coaster I had been absentmindedly mangling. "Oh, I don't know, I'd have to think about it. What about you?" I glanced up, briefly making eye contact once more.

Amber remained completely serious, staring at me without emotion. "No, you wouldn't have to think about it. You know the answer and you don't want to tell me."

I now raised my eyes to stay with hers, fully embracing her piercing gaze. The smile vanished from my face. As far as I could tell, she wasn't kidding, and I was done giving her the benefit of the doubt. "Er, I don't want to be rude, but that's simply not true."

She continued staring at me intently, and I could have sworn that I saw the hints of a grimace creeping across her visage. "Yes it is." Her words were definitive, her tone final.

I turned back to my drink, my eyes double the size they were moments before. "Um ... okay." I took a long, hard pull from my Guinness.

Let's time-out for a minute. I think a person experienced with dating would have thrown the towel in right there, but as this was my first adult date, for all I knew this was the standard operating procedure. Perhaps this was a typical vetting.

Unfortunately, the more I tried to get her to talk and interact, the less she made sense. She went from one highly alarming opinion to another, and after an hour and a half I was getting worn out.

"I just don't see how you can say that Bolivia isn't a real place. Are you saying this is a conspiracy? I mean, how can you believe that? Is this a joke? Are you messing with me?" My voice was growing loud and exhausted, my head in my hands.

She didn't reply, and I took this opportunity to clear my thoughts. "I'm going to the bathroom."

I stood up and walked to the toilet. Once inside, I started frantically mass-texting my friends.

"NEED HELP! DATE IS ACTING WEIRD NOT SURE IF SHE'S TESTING, KIDDING, OR CRAZY."

I waited for replies, but after a few minutes none had come. After what seemed as long as a person could reasonably be gone for, I went back out to the bar and sat down. I took a deep breath as I prepared for round two. "Hey, Amber. I'm back."

Amber looked up at me from her beer. For the first time that evening, she had a grin on her face.

I looked back at her, slightly confused. "What's up?"

Laughter erupted from her. Loud, raucous, unbridled laughter. The surprise nearly caused me to lose my balance on the stool, and she was struggling to maintain hers. I looked at the bartender, thoroughly bewildered. He shrugged, continuing to wipe down his mug. After a minute, Amber tried to speak.

"You just ... have ... no idea." She continued laughing, unable to properly talk.

I looked back at her, silently frowning.

She wiped a tear from her eye. "You have no idea that I'm laughing at you."

I sat for a moment, digesting her words. I contemplated replying, but I could think of nothing to say. Her laughter continued, and after a minute I saw no other option than to leave. Realizing that I had paid up front, I stood up, grabbed my jacket, and walked to the door. My hands shook as I pushed my way out.

By the time I got back to my car, my whole body was shaking. I could barely get the keys in the ignition before tears welled up in my eyes. When Stella and I broke up just two weeks earlier, I was optimistic—the world was my oyster! I would be strutting the streets as the "king of dating" in no time. But in those two short weeks of frustrated swiping, the gravity and reality of the world I lived in came down upon me with the thundering force off Hephaestus's hammer. I was alone, humiliated, and hurt. The void felt endless.

It took me almost twenty minutes to calm down enough to drive. Once I collected the puddle that was my emotionally drained self, I had this sinking feeling that it was only the start of what was to come. Two weeks of swiping, and this is what I had to show for it? Is this what all adult dating would be like?

Fortunately, the answer was not a definitive yes, as the next day offered some hope. A few more matches trickled in, at a pace that would rapidly accelerate as people responded to my interest. But the equation remained the same: I had to extract the dates from the matches like the juice from a lemon, and all I got were short, painfully sour interactions at bars. Even the *notion* of physical romance was beyond consideration; I could barely keep a conversation going.

For example, on my next date, I met a girl at a jazz bar in downtown Seattle, and it was clear from the moment I sat down that she had no interest in me. But that didn't stop her from ordering a few drinks at my expense. It happened again with a different person at a sports bar in Belltown. I made a rule: no more bars.

But changing the location didn't change the equation. I took a girl for a trip to the Olympic Art Park, but she was just looking for friends. I met up with a gal for some Greek food at the Belltown Cafe; she wasn't feeling the spark. I rode a ferry with a girl to Bainbridge Island, but she didn't feel like we were at the same place in our lives.

As these failures piled up, I started asking myself some hard questions. Was I a terrible first date? Was I targeting the wrong kind of people? Did I smell bad? Surely I wasn't *that* ugly, was I? I turned to my male friends—mostly coworkers—and found that it wasn't just me. All of us were struggling to find reasonable, interested people who were also single. What could be causing this phenomenon? Were we all unattractive?

To answer this question, I turned to an old friend of mine for help: science. More specifically, I did a deep dive into U.S. Census data and Pew Research studies. Over the next few weeks, I redirected the energy I had spent swiping on Tinder and turned it to reading papers on demographics and studying population statistics. Surely, I thought, this type of dating experience couldn't be normal. This must be the product of ... well ... something! And my hunch would prove correct.

As I collected data, a clear pattern emerged: the West Coast of the United States was a huge sausage fest, especially the cities of Seattle, San Diego, and of course, Silicon Valley. I was competing with a gigantic number of single dudes for scant few single women. I suspected the reason was the very thing that had brought me here to begin with: the West Coast was full of software engineers, and software engineers are overwhelmingly men. (For those who want a more concrete examination of this theory, look at Secret Bonus Chapter A at the back of the book. It's full of brain-melting analysis that is sure to get any data scientists reading this book hot and bothered.)

To make matters worse, since we software folks were about as common as dirt in these cities, this also made us about as attractive. There's a saying around Silicon Valley and Seattle that captures this, and it goes: "Anyone interested in dating an engineer already is." Plus, how interesting is something that is extremely common? Not very interesting, that's how.

So, what was a man in my position to do? One option would have been to pack my bags and move to Memphis, Tennessee. After all, per the data, it was hands down the best city to find young women.

However, another promising apple had caught my eye: the magical land of New York City. Unlike Memphis, it offered a favorable gender ratio while also having its own little tech mecca known as Silicon Alley, which meant that I would have ample job opportunities. Plus, it seemed like a cool place to live.

All I could do for my final two weeks before moving to San Diego was tell my roommate, Victor, about how amazing the land of New York City was. One night, while we were cooking burgers together on the barbeque, I spouted exposition nonstop. My face was forged in a grin of fervent excitement at my new revelation.

"I'm telling you, Victor, the streets of New York are paved with women." I had a spatula in my left hand, and I gestured wildly as I spoke. Burger juice became airborne and sprayed all over Victor.

Grimacing, Victor wiped the splatter off his face and grabbed the spatula from me. "That's horrifying."

My filibuster continued. "Not literally! One of my friends living there said you can't go ten feet without bumping into a woman."

I was still waving my hands, and Victor kept a close eye on my proximity to the grill. He took his newly acquired flipper and checked the firmness of the patties, speaking unenthusiastically. "Colin, it's New York. You can't go two feet without bumping into *ten* people. Plus, aren't you moving to San Diego in, like, two weeks anyway?"

I continued unimpeded. "Do you think girls pick up guys in bars there? I bet they do ... "

"Look, I really don't know, man." Victor shook his head, flipping the patties carefully.

"I'll bet the girls in New York message first on Tinder. Can you imagine that?" I scratched my chin, nodding thoughtfully.

"That's enough!" Victor threw the spatula down forcefully. "I'm sick of hearing all this talk of your 'Promised Land'! If it's so great, why are you moving to San Diego and not there?"

The patio got quiet. My eyebrows raised, and an even broader grin crossed my face. "Promised Land?" I rubbed my chin thoughtfully. "Yeah. I like the sound of that. We must make a pilgrimage to the Promised Land, Victor! Let us cast away our possessions and go forth to the land of plenty!"

Victor put his hands in his face. "Oh no."

From then on, the magical city of New York would forever be known as the Promised Land. It was a panacea to all male dating problems. I became a prophet of this new religion, and whenever one of my friends would lament his romantic struggles, I would begin my sermon.

With all this talk about New York, you might think that I said "screw it" to the whole San Diego game designer thing, moved to New York, and found love. Or you might think that upon discovering the towering odds stacked against me, I would have at least thrown in the towel on dating while I lived in such a skewed dating market. After all, why waste my time on a lost cause when I could move to the Promised Land later?

Well, remember how I broke up with my girlfriend of four years to pursue a career in video game development? I had a dream. And if that meant sacrificing everything else to make it happen, so be it. Furthermore, even if the dating deck was stacked against me, it didn't mean I was doomed to a lonely life. Rather, I saw this as a challenge, and I relished the opportunity to prove that I could overcome the odds. Besides, even if I failed at love, at least I would keep my skills sharp for my future New Yorker self. What did I have to lose?

The Spider and the Walrus

L ET'S SUMMARIZE THINGS up to this point: after a couple of months being single in Seattle, I eventually came to terms with the fact that my dating life was going to be an uphill battle, in the snow, with most of my limbs either tied behind my back or outright cut off. (Take note, future West Coast curmudgeons: when we're crotchety old grandpas this will make a great "back in my day" story!) But instead of quitting, I decided to up my game. If my previous efforts had been fervent, I was now on maximum overdrive. And as I prepared to move south down the coast of men, I also began to hone my strategies in dating.

First, I revamped my online dating efforts. Rather than spending all of my time blindly swiping through Tinder, I instead set my sights on the dating site OkCupid. Unlike Tinder's minimalistic approach to matching people, OkCupid encouraged users to create rich and detailed profiles. This made it a prime target for developing standardized scripts to improve my match rate. Fortunately, I found a slew of books from mathematicians and data scientists on just how to do this, with titles like *Optimal Cupid: Mastering the Hidden Logic of OkCupid* and *Data Mining: Practical Machine Learning Tools and Techniques*. What had started out as a blind, brute-force hunt for love was turning into a computer-guided search.

Much to my delight, the results of this approach were immediately apparent. Whereas originally I had only been matched with a dozen people, with the help of a few rudimentary scripts I was matched with hundreds. And more important, I was better able to identify interesting users. I found a cluster of young, college-educated women in their twenties—a group that I called "hygiene" because in overwhelming numbers they brushed their teeth twice a day—and decided to optimize my profile for that group.

Now, if this algorithmic approach to dating seems kind of heartless, let me put the issue to rest: it absolutely is! Please excuse me while I tap my fingers together evilly and let out a menacing cackle while lightning strikes through a large plate glass window behind me.

But online dating was only one-half of the equation. I also wanted to improve my ability to meet women through typical in-person encounters. Before the Internet, this was how everyone met, and I certainly wasn't about to limit my options.

To keep this simple, I came up with just one rule: I needed to maximize the number of women whom I asked out on a first date. After all, the best way to find out if someone is a good match is to go on a date with them. And to go on a date, someone must ask for it!

That said, actively trying to close in this manner is not strictly necessary, as you can get to know people through friendship as well. But I couldn't come up a compelling reason to break from this guideline during chance encounters, mainly because there might not be another opportunity for us to meet. The only question that remained was how to go about doing the asking. After much thought, I realized that I only had two options: I could be either a spider or a walrus.

First, let's talk about spiders (said no one, ever). Being a spider, or "spidering" as I like to call it, begins innocuously enough. You meet a girl you like, so you express interest. She's not biting though— maybe she has a boyfriend—but rather than press the issue to a negative conclusion, you decide to wait. You become friends with her. You hang out with her. You start with nothing and slowly weave a sticky web around her life.

As with real spiders, sometimes the butterfly never gets caught in the web. Or perhaps it does, but it breaks away, destroying the web in its desperate attempt to flee. And other times the forces of nature destroy the web before it can ever capture its quarry.

But there are times when the butterfly does get ensnared. First its legs get stuck. Then the wings. The more it struggles the more entangled it becomes. Eventually the spider comes over and wraps up its prey, the circle of life coming to its visceral conclusion.

I was reasonably confident that this is how 100% of marriages ended up happening, and I still am. (I'm not sure this is even an exaggeration.) If this seems like a totally strange thing to say, let me highlight it with an example, involving my friends Tessa and Adam.

Tessa and Adam met in college. Adam was immediately interested in Tessa, but Tessa was not interested in Adam. One night after a toga party, Adam offered to escort Tessa home. Halfway to her dorm, Adam drunkenly stumbled in for a kiss, but Tessa dodged the advance, both literally and metaphorically. The two kept hanging out and became friends, although Tessa was careful to make it clear that Adam was *just* a friend.

However, everything changed one night when Adam was in Tessa's dorm room and they'd both been drinking. Rather than going home, Adam decided to go to sleep in Tessa's bed. Tessa was too tired to care, and so she lay down with him (very romantic, no?). Eventually one thing led to another, and now they are a married couple.

Okay, so you might be thinking, "I know a couple just like this!" And if you are, let me tell you that I am not the slightest bit surprised. I have heard this story a dozen times.

However, the one thing that no one will tell me is what exactly "one thing leads to another" means. Like, how does that happen? Can someone please explain this to me? Does the guy make the first move? Or is it the girl? Do they grind on each other in bed until eventually they go for it? Are they facing each other? Also, aren't the beds in college too small for two people to sleep on comfortably? And what happens if you pull the bed trick too soon, or she isn't going for it? I'm just totally unclear on how this scenario plays out, and I can imagine a million ways for it to go wrong.

The other thing I can't figure out is why this tends to result in long-term, stable relationships that end in marriage. It's truly staggering the number of times I have heard a married person say, "Yeah, they were pretty persistent, and eventually I was like 'meh, all right,' and the rest is history." I guess this is the definition of the word "settling." Or maybe, this is an example of people realizing that they finally have someone they can drag to *Mamma Mia! The Musical.* (I mean, who else are you going to cajole?) God, I need a glass of scotch after writing this.

In any case, that is the spider. Next up we have the other archetype for male-initiated dating: the walrus.

For a moment, I would like you to imagine that you are a woman (this should be a bit easier for the ladies reading this). You are single and you live on a beach. As an unbetrothed, beach-dwelling lass, you naturally enjoy long walks on said beach, and on one of these walks, on a day not particularly different from any other, you hear a splash. You turn to face the water, and as you do, a gigantic sea creature emerges from the surf and comes floundering up onto the sand. Before you even have time to react, the blubbery behemoth stops but a few feet away and lets out an earthshaking roar: "Hey, baby, you want to come over to my place?"

Indeed, this is the walrus. It's the kind of thing that appears from nowhere and does not hide its intentions. It's loud, it's crass, and it knows what it wants (specifically to talk of many things— chiefly eating your clam). This type of approach tends to elicit a much stronger reaction. Some women continue walking along the beach and ignore it. Others might tell it off, or run in fear. And yet, some will be entranced by his mesmerizing call. You might think this sounds ridiculous, but in many situations, it is the norm—such as picking up women at bars. Indeed, the one-night- stand scene is truly rife with these marine mammals. (It's also worth noting that this technique borders on, if not outright is, harassment and is super douchey to women.)

Of course, this needs an example, and I will happily provide. Let me introduce you to Jerry. What's that? He already introduced himself? Well, that's Jerry for you.

But seriously, Jerry and I went to college together. Upon graduation, we both found ourselves in want of a partner for a backpacking trip through Europe. Since we were friends, it seemed like a perfect match. Indeed, the trip went exceedingly well and our summer-long excursion was nothing shy of a fabulous experience.

However, Jerry was single during the trip. And as a single man traipsing across a new continent, he was of course enchanted by the foreign beauties he met along the way. A typical person like me might chat with them and see if there is some chemistry, and if things are going extraordinarily well, might try to make a move. Jerry is not a typical person. Rather, his approach went more like this:

Jerry would begin by walking up to an unsuspecting young woman and saying, "Hi there. I think you're really cute."

The woman would respond, unsure what was going on, "Oh … why, thank you."

Jerry would smile, making friendly eye contact. "I just want to say that I like you a lot, and I would really like to make out with you. Do you want to make out with me?"

Usually the woman's expression would transform to one of complete shock. "Umm, what?"

Many conversations began exactly like this. In most cases, there wasn't even a moment to get in formalities such as names.

You might imagine that this approach is about as effective as asking a rock to make out with you—it's not going to work and you are going to look stupid or insane. But on this trip, it not only worked once, it worked several times. Usually when it did, the women would either just go for it right then and there, or ask a question like "Why are you doing this?" before making out with him. Worse yet, I had no model for who would say yes. Women who I was *certain* would turn him down one minute would be swapping gum with him the next. Not unlike the marvels of Europe (and often not exclusive to), it was truly a sight to behold. (I would like to note that this only works if you are PRETTY DARN good looking. If you look like a troll, you're dead in the water.)

At this point, you might be thinking, "Colin, this is ridiculous. Even if I agree that the spider and the walrus are two ways of going for a girl, they certainly can't be the only two!" Oh, really? Let me prove you wrong.

Say that you are a guy and you meet a girl that you are interested in. (For interest that develops during a friendship, once you decide you want to go for her, we shall, for the sake of this model, call the point where you meet her.) Okay, you have two choices—you can either express that interest immediately and directly (the walrus) or sit on that interest and wait (the spider).

"But Colin!" you cry. "What if you are just a little into her and only hint at interest?"

Sure, that's a thing you could do. And it's a stupid idea. Here's why: if you're not clear with your intentions, now she is guessing. "Is he expressing interest in me or not?" she wonders. You did not make it clear, so you effectively exist in a superposition of walrus and spider states. Eventually, she will either decide that you were expressing interest, just badly, and you are a crappy walrus, or she will decide that you weren't expressing interest, which means you are now someone who is interested in her but not showing it, which is a spider. Since you were not obvious, she got to be the one to make the decision, and worse yet, you probably won't even find out what animal you are! Plus, this confusion is altogether frustrating and exhausting for her, and frankly she doesn't need that kind of stress in her life. She's a person too, you know.

Now, with all this talk of spiders and walruses, you might be wondering what approach I chose. And if I am being perfectly honest, they both seemed unappealing and weird, and made me sour to the whole idea of asking people out at all. But I remained determined, and decided that if I was interested in a girl, I would ask her out at the earliest convenience. And although this is undoubtedly a walrus approach, it didn't seem nearly as crazy as trying to make out with someone on the spot. A walrus I would be, but as polite a walrus as I could manage.

Of course, a theory is no good if it can't withstand criticism, so before I put it into action, I flew it by everyone I knew. And almost everyone—or everyone who hadn't been on the dating scene for a while—asked me why I couldn't just be myself and find love that way. Usually this went along the lines of, "I believe there is a match for everyone, and if you just be yourself I am sure you will find your soulmate." Of course, at the time, I boldly rejected this sentiment as flat-out false—and rightly so! It's totally bogus!

Now, I know this viewpoint is probably going to arouse some skepticism, but please stay with me while I come at this from a few different directions. Like throwing a plate of spaghetti at a wall, hopefully something will stick.

First, let me address the notion of a "soulmate." In addition to being delightfully romantic, the concept is predicated on the idea that each person has one perfect match out there. In other words, for the concept of "soulmate" to be valid, there needs to be *exactly one* partner for which each person is destined. But if each person has one partner, then you need an equal number of straight men and women for such a pairing to exist.

As it turns out, the ratios between men and women aren't equal, no matter how you slice it. Gender ratios tend to be the most heavily skewed at the city level, meaning you end up with a lot of leftover people of one gender. Thus, many are stuck without a soulmate. And since not everyone has a soulmate, the advice to wait for one must be incorrect, because you can't say for sure if the person being advised even has one. (For the curious, reasoning along this line follows a bizarrely named property of mathematics called the "pigeonhole principle," which states that if you have n holes and more than n pigeons, then each pigeon can't get its own hole. It's just one of many examples of why mathematicians shouldn't be allowed to name things.)

Okay, so each person having a soulmate might *technically* be impossible, but for the sake of argument, let's say that somehow it works out anyway. Well, remember how the soulmate model of love requires that each person has exactly one other person with whom they are a good match? Well, this ignores the fact that some people are just objectively more attractive and therefore will match with more than one person.

To see this on a small scale, let's imagine that through the magic of Tesla coils I can exactly copy myself twice, as I am this moment. Let's have one of these Colin copies continue to act like I do today, and the other Colin copy will not take showers or brush his teeth. Also, the second copy will make a bunch of racist and anti-Semitic remarks whenever possible, all while spewing pro-Hitler nonsense.

Now, if we were to poll every woman in my hometown as to which Colin they would rather date, overwhelmingly they would pick the one who doesn't smell terrible and isn't a Nazi. Sure, there might be a few people who like Nazi Colin, but since Nazi Colin is otherwise the same person as real Colin, then I can speak with authority in saying that even Nazi Colin is not a fan of people who like bigots. Ultimately, there is no reason we cannot extend this model to comparing different people, not just varying degrees of Colin, and thus, it doesn't make sense to say that everyone is equally attractive. And since some people are just more attractive than others, the idea of a "soulmate" is broken, because it assumes each person has only one good match.

Now you may not be fully convinced by this reasoning, but I was. And I landed on the following conclusion: I shouldn't be afraid to make changes to myself, or my approaches, to make myself more attractive for dating. And if improving myself meant computationally optimizing my dating profiles and more deliberately asking people out, then that's what I was going to do. As I saw it, even without all the Nazi-clone nonsense, everyone had some degree of Hitler in them, and it's the process of exorcising that Hitler that makes us better people. And by that same token, I wasn't looking for a mythical soulmate: I was looking for someone who, on average, I could tell facts to about Bolivia or drag to *Mamma Mia!* and have them be as excited about these things as I was. I was looking for *neither* of us to have to settle.

The Life of a Rockstar

ABOUT THE TIME I was refining my approach to dating, I moved to San Diego, where I was more than ready to embrace my life as a game designer at the highly successful and well-known company Rockstar Games. Sure, I had given up the love of my life and would be moving to a city where I didn't have any friends or connections, but this would be worth it, right? I was living the dream!

Well, not exactly. There were, unfortunately, some additional drawbacks to taking a job at Rockstar San Diego that I have not mentioned yet. Let's rewind the tape a bit. Over the four months preceding my offer to work at Rockstar—that is, the summer and early fall of 2014—I applied to every English-speaking game studio in the world that had over a hundred employees. And even though I had game-coding experience, I didn't have any professional game *design* experience. Thus, I didn't get a lot of callbacks. In that entire time, I only got five interviews.

As you might have guessed, one of these interviews was at Rockstar. Oddly enough, they were going to interview me for a midlevel design position, as opposed to entry level. Given my lack of applicable work history, this puzzled me, and no matter how I sliced it, I couldn't make sense of it. The day before I flew out for an interview, on a cool day in October of 2014, I asked Derek, a coworker whom I had been discussing dating algorithms with at Microsoft, for an answer as to why this might be.

Derek is, in many respects, a very similar human to myself. Like me, he was an engineer with closeted game design dreams, which we would share while hanging out in the bars of Seattle. He also struggled with finding women to date, but had the one advantage of being a bit smoother with the ladies than I was. (Hold up, I need to amend that. He also had better hair, which was dirty blond, curly like you wouldn't believe, and perfectly complemented his slightly narrow eyes, which gave the impression of deep wisdom. My hair was ultra-straight and brown, and no amount of styling or gel would keep it from flopping back in my face.) Physically, we were both kind of average size and weight, landing around five foot eleven with normal builds.

On this night, we were sitting at the counter in the trendy bar Capitol Cider, a local hot spot that is positively jamming any night of the week. This basement locale has a pair of polished wood shuffleboard tables, an odd thing to find outside of a cruise ship or retirement community, but nonetheless an increasingly common item in the Seattle nightlife. It was this oddity which had enticed us to pay a visit.

Unfortunately, the demand for shuffleboarding was high, so we sat at the polished wooden bar while we waited our turn. The two of us each nursed a large glass of cider as we mulled over our dismal dating prospects. I turned to Derek, swirling my drink nervously. "So, why do you think I got this interview for a midlevel design position at Rockstar? It just doesn't add up."

Derek shook his head knowingly, taking a long swig from his hard cider. "Because it's Rockstar Games, dude."

I looked at him quizzically and raised an eyebrow. "I don't follow."

Derek pulled his phone out of his pocket and punched at it with his thumbs. After a minute, he slid it over to me. "Here. Rockstar San Diego, right?"

I nodded and looked down at the phone, where he had pulled up Glassdoor, a Yelp-like website where employees review employers. It showed Rockstar San Diego with a score of 1.7 out of 5.0. (1.0 is the lowest value.)

I shook my head in disbelief. "Holy cow. How is a score that low even possible?"

Derek shrugged. "Look, man, we both know that the video game industry is notorious for underpaying, overworking, and mistreating their employees. These guys are like the game industry of the game industry. The studio has a reputation. A bad one. People don't want to work there. If you take that job, it's going to be rough."

I flicked through the reviews. People reported arbitrary firings, insane hours, sexual harassment, and employee mistreatment as commonplace events. If HR violations were a bingo game, the reviews made it look like Rockstar San Diego was playing to win blackout. Microsoft, with its cushy benefits and generally amicable environment, seemed like a veritable heaven by comparison.

Let's hold up for a second. For those unfamiliar with and somewhat confused by this casual acceptance of such terrible working conditions in the video game industry, let me give you a brief overview of supply-and-demand economics. Jobs in video games are highly prized, and you won't meet a software professional who doesn't harbor at least some dream of eventually having one. Indeed, I was no exception to this trend. Unfortunately, as in most entertainment fields, the number of people who want to work in it far outstrips the demand for workers.

But instead of the canonical invisible hand rebalancing the equation, this is more like an invisible fist. To rectify the dramatic imbalance between the number of people who want to work in the industry and how many people the industry needs, jobs in games end up being some of the lowest-paying and highest-hours-worked areas in software, because there are many people willing to make those kinds of sacrifices to work on something they love. Additionally, since it's so easy to replace people in the games industry, there is no incentive for businesses to treat their employees well, leading to much worse working conditions than in the broader software industry. (And given how many dudes are on the West Coast, it kind of makes you wonder if the same holds for relationships there, no?)

But even though Rockstar looked bad by the dismal standards of the industry, I decided to fly out for an interview. Worst-case scenario, it would be a micro-vacation. The weather in Seattle in early fall was nothing short of miserable—it was cold, cloudy, and raining. By contrast, San Diego would be splendid. The forecast predicted seventy degrees and a perfect blue sky.

After hopping on the next flight to SoCal, I arrived at the office complex where Rockstar occupied a floor. Nothing seemed out of the ordinary—it appeared to be a very standard office. After I was given the grand tour, they plopped me into a conference room where various interviewers filed in and out through the day. The interviews themselves were unremarkable—mostly involving typical toy questions about how to implement various game systems and design mechanics. However, the final interview with the studio head—a short, bearded, balding man named Jacob—was anything but normal.

Immediately upon walking through the door and before he had even taken a seat, Jacob began speaking. "Okay, so I'm here to convince you not to take this job."

I blinked. "I'm sorry?"

Jacob sat in the office chair directly across from me, continuing his speech. "I'm sure you have heard stories about what it's like here. It's definitely a cult mentality, and either you fit it or you don't."

I shuffled a copy of my résumé around nervously. I wasn't entirely sure if this was a test, so I tried to remain unperturbed. "Um, well, I mean, I don't have a family or anything so I am happy to work long hours. I am really looking to cut my teeth, and it seems like you guys mean business."

Jacob nodded and made eye contact. "That's good. That's good. I want to make sure you know what you are getting yourself into. We have a very specific kind of culture here. This isn't just a job—it's a family. That means if someone invites you to get a drink you don't say no, understand?"

I nodded my head, looking back at Jacob quizzically. Noticing my curious expression, he leaned back in his rolling chair and started an explanation. "There were some guys who did not understand. It didn't end well. Don't make the same mistake. Do you have any questions about all of this? Don't hold back—ask me anything." He leaned forward onto the table that separated us and made solid eye contact once more.

I met his gaze with my own. "Just one. I heard that you throw chairs at people. Is that true?"

Jacob leaned back again and spun around, letting out a sigh. "Let's be clear, I never hit anyone with a chair. I slammed it into a wall during a meeting."

I raised my eyebrows in surprise. "Really?"

"Yes, really." He smirked. "But don't worry, that's not something you'll have to worry about until you become a team lead."

At this point he stood up, thanked me for my time, and left the room. I was a little shocked that he had been so open with me. Our time together had felt like a whirlwind, but I respected his honesty. At Rockstar, it seemed like people were passionate and a little bit temperamental, but not dangerous. His description of Rockstar as a "cult mentality" and "family" gave me the distinct impression that professionalism was a secondary priority, as these phrases carried connotations of casual and unorthodox workplace behavior.

I flew home that evening. I was at the end of my search process; I only had three offers total, and my options were Blizzard Entertainment, Grinding Gear Games (they make a great game by the name of Path of Exile and are based in New Zealand), and Rockstar San Diego. While all of those seemed promising, the first two were offering me very low salaries, and I technically hadn't finished the final round of interviews at Blizzard, although I was told that I'd done rather well up to that point and would probably get an offer. As I had grown quite fat and happy on my cushy Microsoft engineer salary (the golden handcuffs, as they say), I was reluctant to take a pay cut of 75% to work at either of the first two companies. However, I would only be taking about a 50% pay cut to work for Rockstar, plus I would be nonexempt-salaried, meaning I would make overtime for anything beyond forty hours. Given what the Glassdoor reviews said about the crazy amount people worked, it seemed like I wouldn't even be making much of a monetary sacrifice. To boot, I would be a midlevel game designer, which would be a huge step in the direction I wanted to go.

In the days after my interview, I thought hard about the decision I would be making. Was it the right choice to go somewhere that had employee reviews that were almost half that of notorious companies like Walmart (3.1) and Walgreens (3.0)? (By comparison, Microsoft landed at a cool 3.9.)

As I weighed my options, I kept returning to one thought: I was not a designer at Microsoft, I was an engineer. It had been made very clear I would never be able to make that transition. Could I sell out my dream and stay at Microsoft? In the back of my mind, my inner voice kept saying: "If you become a designer now, someday you're going to be the J. J. Abrams of video games. People will turn to you and say, 'Colin, we need your brilliance to make Star Wars great again!' And you will wave to the crowd, gladly accepting the mantle (and hopefully cape and crown!) as the savior of humanity."

And with that, I decided to go. I figured that if I could survive the gauntlet that awaited me in the sunny land of San Diego, I could move on to bigger and better things in a few years. Also, as pretentious as it sounds for me to say it, another thought crossed my mind: "I'm a white male." While I would have to put up with the shitty hours and pay, the alleged sexual harassment and discrimination didn't apply to me.

I accepted the offer the next day, immediately after it was formally extended. It took me all of four minutes to sign and return the electronic contract from when it hit my inbox.

The moving process itself was uneventful. I found an aerospace researcher who was renting a room with a private bath just a mile and a half from Rockstar, and I packed all my belongings and drove down the coast. In but a few weeks from the interview, I was stepping into my first days as a video game designer. To be precise, it was November 17, 2014, two days before my twenty-fourth birthday. A good omen, to be sure.

The large office was L-shaped. It had a high ceiling and an open floor plan that seated around two hundred engineers, designers, and artists. My team was in the corner, right next to the central kitchen and bathrooms. I met my coworkers, all of whom were in their twenties like me. They all seemed reasonably cool, but I got along with one person particularly well, a guy by the name of Shen. It was one of those moments where you meet someone and you just know that you two are going to be friends. He was a soft-spoken, Southeast Asian, twenty-three-year-old Hearthstone player with long black hair who by some strange coincidence had gone to school with and knew the very Derek I had been friends with at Microsoft.

Even from just the first day on the job, I found that, compared to being an engineer, being a game designer was exactly what I wanted. Instead of worrying about how to make the game run, I would be spending my time figuring out how to make multiplayer system fun and intuitive while still being realistic to develop. Ahead of me lay all kinds of fascinating problems, including user-interface design, player spawning, and character abilities.

I also realized that I had no shortage of ideas for how to make the game better—there was simply a shortage of time for *implementing* the ideas. Suddenly, I had an opportunity to exert my creativity on the game. All I had to do was stay at work a bit longer each day to make sure my ideas made the cut. And best of all, I would get paid overtime for it.

About halfway through my first week, on my birthday, I received an email about an event that was being held by the design team to celebrate the arrival of three new designers—two other ones and myself. We were going to meet at Beachside Bar and Grill, located in the nearby town of Encinitas, that coming Friday night.

On Friday morning, I was approached by one of the administrators of the office, Alysia, who wanted to introduce me to some of the important people at the company—mostly team leads and directors. One of the people I met was named Damon, and he was one of the many vice presidents at Rockstar Games. He was a warm and lively guy, and was also squat and kind of pudgy. He had medium-length tan hair hidden beneath a baseball cap and a clean-cut face. Normally based out of Vancouver, he was visiting our office for the week. I was struck by how friendly he was, as most people only exchanged a few words with me when I was showcased by. In fact, when I stopped by his interim office, he seemed genuinely interested in having a conversation.

Alysia started off the interaction. "Hi there, Damon. I just wanted you to meet our new designer, Colin."

Damon stood up and engaged me with a handshake that couldn't be beat. "It's a pleasure to meet you, Colin. What team are you going to be working on?"

I put my hand down and stuttered a nervous response. "Multiplayer design."

Damon's warm personality smoothed over any apprehension I had about meeting an executive. He maintained eye contact and smiled. "Fantastic. Have you gotten a chance to play the game yet?"

I smiled now too. "Yeah, actually, I just finished playing through the current build. It's much further along than I would expect at this juncture!"

Damon nodded and looked at Alysia, who stood by fidgeting nervously. His tone changed from warm to earnest in an instant. "That's good. That's very good. I've had to fire designers before for not playing the game. Completely unacceptable." He looked back at me, his smile gone.

I was somewhat taken aback by the dramatic turn. The smile vanished from my face, and I looked to Alysia for guidance. She didn't miss the cue. "Well, it was great seeing you again, Damon, but I'm sure you are really busy, so we'll get going now."

Damon waved us out, and we were off.

I made a mental note after that conversation that he seemed somewhat volatile. This concerned me, but as I had already played through the current version of the game, at least I didn't have to worry about getting fired for that.

Eventually evening arrived, and sometime between 8:00 and 9:00 p.m., Shen and I carpooled down from our Carlsbad office to Encinitas. When we arrived at the bar and grill, there were maybe twenty or so people present at a long table located in the outdoor seating area. Things were loud and lively, with people enjoying the free food and drinks. At some point, Damon got up from the head of the table and sat across from me in the middle.

Immediately he made his presence known, interrupting the small talk I had been making with the other new designers. "I am so glad to have a talented person like you joining us." Damon beamed at me as he spoke. "I'm also very impressed that you have already played through the game."

The two other new designers sat on either side of me, and they shifted uncomfortably in their seats. My manager, who was sitting next to Damon, coughed and nodded his head toward them in a not-so-subtle way.

Damon picked up on the hint, leaning back and growing red in the face. "Oh well, Colin just looked so quiet over here, I had to say something to him. These guys seemed to be fine." He waved dismissively at the two other new designers, who were now frowning.

Fortunately, the uncomfortable moment passed and the conversation returned to its previously jovial state. But in the back of my mind, I thought it seemed a little strange that Damon was taking an interest in me specifically. I shrugged the thought away, figuring that earning the favor of an executive could only help my career.

At around 10:00 p.m., just as things were hitting their stride, Damon became quite agitated and abruptly stood up. He looked directly at my manager, who was talking to another design lead. He spoke quietly, but intently.

"Lucas."

"Lucas."

"Hey, Lucas!"

My manager, Lucas, looked up. "Hmmm?"

Damon gave him a knowing look. "It's kind of late, isn't it?"

Lucas paused momentarily, thinking, then responded hurriedly, "Oh yes. It *is* getting late, isn't it? About that time." He stood up and put on his jacket.

The strange interaction was a bit too loud and a bit too wooden, drawing the attention of nearly everyone at the table. Noticing the sea of eyes now fixed on him, Lucas was quick to address the situation. He waved noncommittally, all while slowly edging toward the door with Damon. "Well, I am his ride home." With that, Lucas and Damon left the dining area.

Once they had left, one of the two new designers turned to me, "What just happened?"

I shook my head. "Beats me."

He continued, sighing in frustration as he poked a puddle of ketchup with a cold potato wedge, "Plus, he totally blew us off with that remark to you, Colin. What the hell was that all about?"

I shrugged, making a placating facial expression as I watched him push a glob of honey mustard around his plate. "Man, I have no idea."

The one other new designer interjected. "Whatever. We still get free food and drinks. Don't think too hard about it." I turned to face him, watching him take a long swig of beer. Despite his nonchalant attitude, his mood seemed decidedly down. But after a few minutes and another round of drinks, the three of us resumed enjoying ourselves and continued our prior conversation.

Another twenty minutes later, Lucas stepped back out onto the patio, his face bearing no expression. He walked up to the three of us new designers and got down on one knee, speaking very quietly to avoid attention. "Would you guys mind stepping into the lobby for a photo opportunity with Damon?"

The three of us looked at each other, wide-eyed and silent. The designer to my right broke the quiet. "Where have you been for the last thirty minutes? And why are you back? Didn't you take Damon home?"

Another man at the table, a man whom I vaguely recognized as a design lead like Lucas, stood up and walked over to us. By now, several people had noticed Lucas's mysterious reappearance and were chattering about it around the table.

I looked from one of the new designers to the other. They both seemed unsure. "Uh, yeah, we can come out to the lobby," I hesitantly responded. "Yeah, let's do it."

The five of us—Lucas, the other team lead, the two new designers, and myself—started walking toward the entrance. Lucas headed up the pack, weaving us between noisy, crowded tables as we made our way to the lobby. But we didn't stop there. We went straight through the front doors and started walking down the street.

Confused by the fact that we had clearly blown right past the lobby, one of the other new designers spoke up. "Hey, so where are we going? I thought this was a photo thing at the entrance to the restaurant. Why are we leaving?"

Lucas waved dismissively, his voice slightly irritated. "Just follow us, okay?"

The other new designer laughed nervously. "This is *really* odd."

Noticing the uncomfortable tension, Lucas stopped. His voice was calmer and less annoyed now, although there was still a hint of apprehension. "Okay, so we are going to a nightclub where there is a reserved table with bottle service. Damon wanted to have a smaller setting to get to know you guys. Think of it as a welcome event."

I nodded in understanding. I had heard stories that Rockstar used to initiate new recruits with a trip to a strip club, and this seemed to be a toned-down equivalent of that tradition. But instead of being excited at the upgrade in venue, I was nervous. My two interactions with Damon had shown him to be unpredictable, and the bad vibe I was getting from my manager certainly wasn't putting my mind at ease.

"There is one more thing you need to know," Lucas said nervously as he threw a cautious look at the other design lead. "Be very, very careful what you say to Damon."

I furrowed my brow. "I don't follow."

Lucas continued. "There were some guys in quality assurance that made some less-than-positive remarks about our games. Damon found this upsetting. Don't end up like them. Do you understand?"

The three of us nodded sheepishly. This seemed oddly reminiscent of what Jacob, the studio head, had told me a few weeks earlier during my final interview. I took a deep breath. If I was nervous before, I was positively on edge now.

As we kept walking, the other lead clarified further. "Damon is ... "

He scratched the back of his neck, searching for words. "Just stay on his good side. That's all we are saying."

Let's pause the story for a moment. I want to call attention to the language and repetition that the people in leadership were using regarding the situation we were about to find ourselves in. Never were the consequences explicitly stated, but it was heavily implied that "bad things" would happen if we weren't careful (I think most people would interpret this as getting fired). From what I could tell, both Lucas and the other lead seemed rather uncomfortable about the entire thing, like they were afraid this could go south quickly. I'm sure the fact that everyone had downed a couple of drinks didn't put their minds at ease. And as a new designer who had literally put everything else on hold for this job, I took them very seriously. Keep this in mind as we continue.

After walking a few blocks, we reached a nightclub called Shelter, where we met Damon at a private booth in the back-right corner. We all squeezed onto a U-shaped couch that surrounded a small table covered in glasses and bottles. The club was loud and packed, and on the table sat an assortment of Grey Goose, mixers, and some whiskey. After we all sat down and poured ourselves drinks, a very awkward and tense half hour passed. No one knew what to say, or how to break the ice. The other new designers alternated trying to catch Damon's interest, but neither seemed to be having any luck.

Trying to strike up a more natural conversation, Lucas turned to me. "So tell me about yourself. You have a girlfriend down here?"

Damon, who had been half listening to a story one of the other designers was telling, turned his attention to us. I shook my head. "No, it's just me."

A moment of silence passed and I followed up, "I don't even know anyone here. My closest friends are in Los Angeles. I know one person at UC San Diego. I'm kind of a taking a dive into the deep end. I'm definitely excited, but it's a pretty new experience."

Damon jumped in, leaning close to be heard over the ambient noise of the club. "Why don't you find a nice girl here?" He made a sweeping gesture toward the crowd.

I shook my head. "Nah, not really my thing."

As the words left my mouth, a few people showed up, including Alysia, the person who had first introduced me to Damon, and a third design lead. These two were quite sociable and their presence eased the mood considerably. But as they arrived, my manager, Lucas, inexplicably left. None of this coming and going made any sense to me.

Not long after Lucas left, Damon started looking antsy, like he had at the first restaurant right before he left. He stood up and moved to the end of the table, waving his hands in an upward motion at us. "Come on, guys! Let's party!"

Having been awkwardly pinned to this table for the better part of an hour, I thought that sounded like a smashing idea. I stood up and joined him and said something to the effect of, "Yeah, let's party!"

At this point, Damon grabbed me, pulled himself close, and started grinding on me. He grabbed my ass and ran his hands up and down my body. As suddenly as this paragraph just hit you, dear reader, so was I surprised by what was now happening. I didn't know what to do, and I certainly didn't want to be the guy to test

Damon's temperamental side. So I stood there and let it happen. I tried to force a smile, like it was no big deal, but I was panicking as he held me close and his hands continued to wander. During this, we were still at the end of the table and everyone could see. Alysia was standing right next to me.

Damon at some point stopped and sat down. He pointed at his lap and looked at me; I was unclear if he wanted me to sit on it or give him a lap dance. I looked around sheepishly but no one said anything. The table was dead quiet. I looked back at Damon, who now spread his knees wide, and made a more forceful hand gesture toward his lap. He looked at me insistently.

My chest tightened. My heart pounded in my ears. I once more looked to the faces around the table, only to see everyone staring down at their drinks, a look of deep discomfort shared between them. I had no time to think. Only one thought filled my mind: if I didn't do what he wanted, *whatever that was*, would it cost me my job?

As this thought flooded my brain in the scant few seconds my hesitation afforded, I pragmatically decided that, at the very least, I'd rather not be sitting in his lap, so I turned to face away from him and started giving him a lap dance, avoiding contact as best I could. Shortly after, Alysia told me to stop and I did.

As you can imagine, at this point I felt extremely ashamed and embarrassed, like I have never been at any point before or after in my life. My brain screamed so loud that I couldn't have heard the blaring music had I wanted to. I wanted to cry, to shout, to run, to be *anywhere* but there. I had no sexual interest in men, and that certainly extended to Damon, and doing this in front of everyone I had to work with was intensely humiliating. And although the whole incident couldn't have lasted more than a few minutes, it's something I will never forget. Afterwards, I tried to make small talk with another designer, but the mood was decidedly uncomfortable. Eventually one of the design leads sympathetically motioned for me to sit next to him, and I did. Hands shaking, I poured a very stiff vodka tonic. The design lead, who I found out was named Toby, tried to chat with me, his voice reassuring and calm, but I can only remember staring fixedly at the flock of Grey Goose bottles on the table before me.

After a few minutes, Damon, who had seated himself at the other side of the table, stood up. And as he began to walk over, time came to a stop. Each step passed in slow motion; I could see the laughing faces of the people around me, the spilled drops of vodka and juice on the table, the sequential flashing of each colored light in the club. But only one thought filled my mind: *"Please, do not sit next to me."*

As the moment passed, Damon took a seat on my left and placed his right arm around my shoulders. He put his left hand on my knee. He started rubbing my leg. I remained frozen, continuing to stare fixedly at the Grey Goose bottles in front of me. My hands began shaking more intensely as I clutched my glass tumbler. Toby kept trying to talk to me but I could not say anything. I wanted to scream for Damon to stop, but couldn't. I just sat there, paralyzed. My discomfort was drawing a lot of attention around the table.

Toby looked sternly at Damon. "Cut it out, man."

Damon looked taken aback, making an innocent facial expression. "Whaaat?"

Toby looked at Damon's hand on my knee, and then looked Damon directly in the eyes. "Take your hands off him, Damon." His voice was forceful; there was no mistaking the urgency.

For a full second Damon returned his gaze. Finally, he rolled his eyes and stood up, walking to the other side of the table and letting out an exasperated sigh.

My manager, Lucas, returned a few minutes later. My phone buzzed and I looked at it—it was roughly midnight and I had just received a text from Shen, the designer with whom I carpooled over, who wanted to leave soon. From this brief conversation two messages stand out:

Shen, 12:04 a.m.: "Yeah, I'm here, still a ripcord if you need it."

Me, 12:05 a.m.: "I need it."

Somehow he knew where I was, even though I never told him. I had last seen him at the Beachside Bar and Grill, yet within minutes he was standing next to me in Shelter. Before and since, I have never been so happy to see a fellow human being. I immediately got up to leave with Shen.

As I stood, Damon's face contorted in surprise. "You're leaving now?" He looked miffed.

"Yes," I replied quietly, trying to avoid eye contact. We made eye contact anyway.

He extended his hand.

I extended mine.

He gave me a handshake that couldn't be beat.

Shen and I left the club. We walked back to his car in silence. Once we were in the car and driving, I gave a summary of what had happened. Shen seemed startled, and I suspect he couldn't tell if I was being serious.

After I shared my story, an awkward silence followed. He broke it. "I actually heard that Toby has done similar things." His voice sounded somewhat sad and distant.

I looked to my left, to where he sat in the driver's seat. "Like what?"

He shook his head. "That's all I know."

Eventually he dropped me off at home. I went upstairs to my room, stripped naked, and sat in the shower. I wept. My nearest friends and family were hundreds of miles away; I had left them for this. I had left my well-paid, respectable job as a software engineer at Microsoft for this. I had left my brilliant PhD girlfriend of four years for this. I had left any shred of dignity I had for this. I was living the dream.

The next morning, a Saturday, arrived without sleep. I was required to come to work and went in as requested. But given how I had snubbed Damon the night before, as I approached the locked doors of our office, I wondered if the light on the badge reader would still turn green when I swiped. After all, Damon seemed irked when I left—perhaps that would translate to a rapid departure.

Mercifully, the door opened to my card key. I walked to my desk, where I found little respite as I silently worked. While there, I over-heard another team lead speaking to Lucas. "Yo, I heard some crazy shit went down last night after I left. What the hell happened?"

Lucas shook his head and walked away, glancing at me ever so briefly as he did. "Later."

After work, I continued the conversation with Shen about what had happened, and he quickly realized that I was still very upset over the ordeal. Later that night, Shen told me that he had contacted the studio head, Jacob, and strongly encouraged me to speak with the on-site HR rep.

I thought hard about whether to reach out to HR. If I did, there would be no going back. But I saw few alternatives before me. Con-vinced that Damon would either come back for seconds or see to my eventual dismissal, my best bet seemed to be seeking official protection. The next day, Sunday, I typed up an email, asking HR for help. Oddly enough, the HR rep, Eleanor, said she was in the office, and we agreed to meet at 4:30 p.m.

It took a full half hour to relay the entire story to her, nothing held back. She took notes on a pad of yellow lined paper as I spoke. Finally, I finished, my hands shaking, " ... So that's what happened. I want to be clear that I remember the events of Friday night very clearly despite being intoxicated."

Eleanor nodded. Her face was serious and compassionate. "I have no doubts that this is true; you are being extremely detailed and thorough. I just want to say that I am so sorry for what happened. However, I need to talk to some people, so you'll need to hold on." She paused, looking to her desk as she searched for words. "This is not Rockstar. We're here to make games and that is it. I am shocked to hear of this kind of thing happening."

I narrowed my eyes and looked at her suspiciously. "Really? I'm surprised to hear you say that. Before I left Microsoft, I heard numerous stories about crazy things happening here, which is how I even knew about the whole chair-throwing thing with Jacob. That's not even to mention the Glassdoor reviews."

Eleanor immediately shook her head, her face remaining serious and calm. "I know Damon. He's a good person. I'm sure he was going through a difficult time, or some deep emotional crisis."

A lump formed in my throat as I looked back at her calm expression, unable to process what I had just heard. In an attempt to protect myself and call attention to what I saw as an obviously endemic issue, I hadn't even considered what Eleanor's role in this might be. But the moment she tried to excuse away the behavior instead of condemning or denying it, I became convinced that I was just the latest link in a chain of events that she was already keenly aware of. (To be clear, I am not implying that she was in cahoots with Damon or anyone else on this. More likely, I suspect that she simply was too close to these people to act as an unbiased judge.)

I sat quietly, in slow acceptance of the company I had willfully joined. Calmly, Eleanor closed out the conversation. "Come to work tomorrow and try to move forward. I'll be in touch."

The next day she sent an email which informed me that HR had opened an investigation. However, as the days passed, they also told me that none of the people present would corroborate my side of the story—not even Toby, who had publicly rebuked Damon. In the end, it was my word against Damon's, and HR recommended that Damon and I *sit alone together in a room* to talk things out. (It baffles me that they thought the solution to alleged sexual harassment is to put the two parties alone in a room together.) When I prickled at the suggestion, the now two HR representatives involved alternated between offering wild explanations for his behavior and stating that I was making the whole thing up, with reasoning such as, "Well, he *is* married and has a wife, so your story doesn't make any sense."

I no longer felt comfortable or safe at work. And as the weeks and months passed, I resolved to leave Rockstar. But before I did, there was one person I needed to speak with.

A week before my last day, I arranged for Toby, the design lead who had told Damon to take his hands off me, to meet me in a conference room one-on-one, hoping to understand why he wouldn't go on the record about his intervention at the nightclub. Of course, I was grateful, but I was also more than a little frustrated that he had decided to keep quiet.

As I closed the door to the room, I dispensed with the pleasantries. "You know why I asked you to meet, yeah?"

Toby nodded. "I have a pretty good idea."

I nodded back. "So why didn't you say anything to HR? They told me they talked to you."

Toby wore a stern expression, replying in a quiet, serious voice as he took a seat in a swivel chair. "I think it's best if we all move forward and forget this happened."

I frowned, crossing my arms. "Easy for you to say. Are you worried you are going to get fired? What gives?"

Toby sighed. "I think it's best if we all move forward and forget this happened."

I frowned more intensely now. "I see."

Toby stood up, his face still serious. "Anything else?" He walked over to the door, pausing with his hand on the handle. I shook my head and he left.

Sadly, this wasn't all that happened in the short five months I spent at Rockstar. In addition to regularly being expected to work six days a week, I got to witness all except one women's bathroom get converted to men's rooms (much to the chagrin of the one woman on my team), people smoking weed *inside* the office building, and fistfights at the Christmas party.

Truly, Rockstar had lived up to its reputation. And if anyone reading this is considering employment at Rockstar, or more generally in the field of video game development, I want to offer some advice. While this experience is extreme, it's not *that* extreme for the games industry. Sexism, sexual harassment, long hours, lack of job stability, and low pay are the norm. (I want to underscore how bad it is for women.) If you think you are immune to that, know that you are not. I don't care if you are a young white male like me. It can happen to you. Maybe you like the idea of being a game designer enough to justify the risk—personally, I did not. It's a cool gig, don't get me wrong, but there is no way in hell I would consider going back to that industry. It may be true that we all just wannabe big rock stars, but living that life comes at a steep price.

Summer Lovin'

UE THE *GREASE* MUSIC! Yep, that's right, it's time for a good ol'-fashioned beach story. If you are mortified by the last chapter's gravity, this one will make you smile with its lightheartedness and joy. In all seriousness, though, this chapter will have some heavier moments, so maybe turn those glasses from rosé to burgundy. All set? Let's do this.

Our story picks up where we left off, in the magical land of San Diego, California. Actually, I need to amend that slightly—I was living about thirty-five miles north of San Diego in a small city called Carlsbad. For those who don't know precisely where that is (which will be everyone who hasn't lived there), it sits a bit south of halfway between Los Angeles and San Diego, on the coast of the Pacific Ocean.

Before we go any further, let me just say that there is *nothing* for a twenty-four-year-old to do in Carlsbad. It's basically a retirement community with a Lego-themed amusement park. The nearest real city is San Diego, a solid forty-five minutes to the south in good traffic. To add to this woeful state of affairs, I knew no one in the area and, as you probably can guess, I hated my job. I was off to a great start!

Thus, with nothing else going for me, I turned my attention back to online dating. By now my optimizations had reached full maturation, and OkCupid was sending me a steady stream of dates. I also returned to Tinder, although with less ferocity than before. I swiped at a solid pace, but not a blistering one. I upgraded my pictures and bio, shedding glasses for contacts. I studied men's fashion and wore better-fitting clothing in my photos. My swipe-to-date ratio improved. I was now going on a date about every four days.

In addition to my looks, the dates themselves got an overhaul. I eschewed long, planned-out romantic escapades in favor of quick chats at ice cream parlors and coffee shops, mostly because I knew how things were going within the first several minutes. This added a sense of routine to my dates, which, to my pleasant surprise, reduced my nervousness around meeting new girls.

Sadly, date after date yielded no success. Mostly they flopped because the girl and I had nothing in common, and after an hour or two we would usually call it quits. But everything changed when I met up with a University of California San Diego graduate student named Kathryn at a bubble tea place just north of campus. She was amused by my ability to country two-step (another story for another time), which is, to the best of my knowledge, why she even wanted a first date to begin with. As an astrophysics PhD student who shared the same favorite animal as my ex (vampire squid), she was as cheerful and bright as my dating life was dismal.

We walked into the bubble tea place, Tapioca Express, at the exact same time. After grabbing our teas, we took seats in a couple of dilapidated red armchairs near the back of the boutique. Immediately we hit it off. Something about her warm demeanor and unbridled exuberance filled me with renewed life. The conversation flowed easily and the awkwardness of meeting someone for the first time vanished almost instantly. As the night grew late and the shop closed, a second date seemed certain. It was only a matter of when and where. A flurry of texts would lead us to a definite conclusion.

Kathryn: "Have a bottle of wine that needs to be put to good use ... "

Me: "Sounds like a great evening activity!"

Kathryn: "Where? If it's nice, we could hike down the Torrey Pines trail and sneak it onto the beach."

Me: "Perfect. I'll bring an opaque water bottle."

Kathryn: "Ha-ha! Date just got a lot classier :P"

Not one to be outdone on the romance-o-meter, I decided to step up my game for the second date. On my way to the beach, I stopped by Safeway and picked up a bag of ice, a knife, and some fancy cheese (okay, it wasn't that fancy, but it was still pretty Gouda). I stuffed these items into my daypack, which already had a bottle for surreptitiously storing our wine and several other essentials. Among these items was a deck of cards, a pair of sandals, eight condoms (better than running out!), and a towel (which is about the most massively useful thing a SoCal beachgoer can have, as it has great practical value). With this level of preparation, I was truly a force to be reckoned with.

Additionally, since the trail parking lot was certain to be full, we decided to meet at the nearby Torrey Pines Golf Course, which sat on an oceanside cliff next to the beach. From there we could amble down the bluffs along the wooden stairs of the Torrey Pines trail and onto the narrow strip of sand between the water and the cliffs.

Conveniently and purely by chance, I parked right next to Kathryn in the lot. I stepped out of my car with my laden bag, and Kathryn's eyebrows shot to the top of her head as she pointed at my back. "What on earth do you have in your pack, Colin? It looks ready to break at the seams!"

I shrugged, keeping cool and smiling amicably. "Beach stuff, of course."

Kathryn shook her head, her mouth half open as she continued staring fixedly at my bulging package. "Whatever you say."

Regardless of any reservations she may have had regarding my equipment, we soon abandoned our cars and trundled off toward the beach. As we made our way along the sandy bluffs, they soon gave way to wooden stairs, which led down the eroding cliffs and toward the golden shore.

While we walked, Kathryn turned and looked at me inquisitively. "So, Colin, I never heard what you did for a living."

I turned to her with sad eyes, sighing as I spoke. "Ah yes. I'm a game designer. That said, I won't be for long. It's terrible, and I can't wait to quit."

Kathryn's interested smile was immediately replaced by a wide-eyed expression of amazement. "Wow, that sounds really cool, though! What are you going to do if you leave?"

I shrugged. "I dunno, probably go back to being a software engineer."

As soon as the words left my mouth I knew I had made a mistake. I had broken the number one rule: Never, EVER, tell women on the West Coast you are a software engineer.

Let's hold up for a moment. It is likely that as my reader you do not hold this truth to be self-evident, and might be wondering, "My good chap, Colin [this is my best attempt imagining what you sound like, so bear with me], I do declare that this statement of yours is most perplexing indeed! Why ever would an upstanding individual such as yourself need to lie about such an aristocratic profession? Surely the damsels must have their knickers properly kinked at a dapper analytical engine circumlocutor such as yourself!" Indeed, such would be the hope, my fellow member of the gentry. But alas, it is not the reality.

Rather, my tenure in Seattle had made me intimately familiar with a widespread disgust of the more computationally oriented folks. Remember how before I made a comment about how software engineers were as common as dirt on the West Coast and therefore about as attractive? Well, there is another factor working against us: a lot of people think engineers are jerks.

This reputation is not entirely undeserved. Indeed, we tend to think we are the smartest thing on two legs, know a lot of facts, and feel a crushing desire to impart those facts upon other people, *especially* if we think they are wrong about something. Mix that with a fat paycheck, and this results in a potent human being who can be fairly summarized as "too big for his britches." The aversion created by these people is so strong, in fact, that many software engineers declare themselves to be of alternative professions to avoid typecasting. Hence, when dating, I was not Colin the engineer, but instead, Colin the architect.

In fact, I had gotten so good at telling people I was an architect that I'd genuinely started believing it to be true. I could snootily cite my gushing love of Christopher Alexander's *The Timeless Way of Building* and comfortably drop into a discussion about the latest Cronenberg creation of master architect Frank Gehry. So long as no one *actually* knew a darned thing about being an architect, I was in the clear.

Sadly, on this day I would no longer be able to deploy such a ruse. My tongue had slipped and my fate was sealed. I waited for a sharp intake of breath, followed by a scream of existential horror.

Instead, Kathryn's tone remained cheerful and excited. Her eyes seemed alight with interest. "Whoa, that's crazy. I don't think I have ever been on a date with a software engineer before. You're basically a computer wizard, right?"

I looked back at her skeptically, struggling to parse the mismatch between her response and the expected scream. "I'm a what?"

"You're a wizard!"

I rubbed my chin, unable to contain a growing smile. "Yeah. I ... I guess I am."

Kathryn grabbed my arm and shook it enthusiastically. "That's really cool!"

I paused, unsure how to respond. My suspicion began to fade, but I still wasn't sure that she wasn't going to scream.

Kathryn continued, "I mean, you can program. You know how valuable that kind of thing is in the sciences? I'm trying to learn some myself—really useful."

I stared back at her blankly, thoroughly stumped. How could such a reaction be possible?

I'll spare you the detailed explanation on demographics, but basically it turns out there are not nearly as many software folks in San Diego as there are along the rest of the Pacific seaboard. Rather, San Diego tends to be populated mostly by marines and other men of martial bearing, which is how it gets its rather stilted gender dynamics to fit in with Seattle and Silicon Valley. (On the East Coast, Virginia Beach suffers the same fate.)

Regardless of the exact cause of this windfall, I was in the clear. Plus, I didn't have to maintain a fake professional identity! As I relaxed, we continued our stair-stepping hike down to the beach, my mood as vibrant as the last light of day.

When we reached the bottom of the stairs, Kathryn leapt forward and shouted excitedly over her shoulder, "I know a good spot! Follow me!"

I followed close behind as she skipped ahead. And as I did, I couldn't help but notice how her hair had the same color as the dark sandstone cliffs, its tight curls whipping playfully in the stiff ocean breeze. Her skin was smooth and tan, matching the color of the soft sands.

After bounding along for a few minutes, we took a turn around a large rocky outcrop that jutted nearly to the waterline. On the other side a sandy cove lay before us, set into the cliffs and rising up above the surrounding beach.

Kathryn turned around, her round, cheerful face one of definite delight as she smiled broadly. "This is perfect! Shall we stop here?"

This seemed as good a spot as any, so I nodded and pulled out a towel to sit on. After we had kicked off our shoes and made ourselves nice and comfy, it seemed the appropriate time to turn on the charm machine.

I reached toward my backpack, shooting Kathryn a suave look. "Would you like some wine, milady?"

Kathryn nodded vigorously, gently placing a hand on my arm. "Of course, my good sir."

"Wunderbar. I was hoping you would say that." I pulled out my metal canteen, unscrewing the cap as I offered her the first sip. As she drank, I reached into the pack and pulled out the knife and cheese.

At this point you are probably thinking that—given how I sold you on this book—something was about to go horribly, horribly wrong. Perhaps the canteen had leaked and was basically empty. Maybe the cheese had melted too. Or maybe my backpack was completely full of spiders (OKAY, NOW *THAT* IS A DISTURBING THOUGHT).

Surely, SURELY, SHIRLEY, something was wrong. But nope, everything was just dandy. We sliced cheese and sipped wine under the emerging stars. It was a glorious evening.

As the sun finally dropped below the horizon and the air cooled, we scooted closer together on the towel. I tossed our empty make-shift wine bottle into the sand and placed an arm around her shoulders. She huddled tight to me to keep warm. Sensing the moment, I leaned in for a kiss, which she responded to in kind. Our lips touched once, and again, and again. We pulled in closer, our bodies warm against the cold night.

I stopped for a moment to speak. "So, what do you say we kick it up a notch?"

Kathryn pulled back, raising one eyebrow and frowning dramatically. "But ... it's so ... PUBLIC!"

I sat up, speaking calmly and collectedly. "Yeah, but it's dark, and who's going to see us? I haven't seen anyone in almost an hour."

Kathryn shifted uncomfortably, looking down at the towel with a slight frown. "I didn't bring any protection, though."

I unzipped the front pocket on my backpack and revealed the condoms.

Kathryn's mouth now was wide open. "WHY ON EARTH DO YOU HAVE EIGHT CONDOMS? WE ARE NOT HAVING SEX EIGHT TIMES."

I laughed. "I just wanted to be prepared, that's all!"

Kathryn nodded absentmindedly, still mortified at the contents of my backpack. "Can we just keep making out? We can go back to your place later and do that."

I nodded, shrugging amicably. "Sure. That seems like a fine idea. No rush."

We returned to making out. However, after about ten minutes, something caught my attention.

I pulled back, looking up at Kathryn confusedly. "Did you just spill something on my feet?"

Kathryn rolled her eyes. "How on earth would I do that ... you're on top of me."

I glanced over at the canteen, which was still sitting empty in the sand a few feet away.

"Then what just got my foot wet?"

As if to answer my question, my pants and the bottom half of the towel suddenly became very, VERY wet. Indeed, Kathryn was not the source of the unpleasantness—the rising tide was.

Kathryn scrambled backward, pointing out at the water. "Colin, look!"

I turned to see that our slightly elevated cove was now the last bit of beach left. On either side of us, rocky protrusions from the tall sandstone cliffs stretched into the water, effectively trapping us on our small section of beach. The narrow sand strip we had taken to get to our location was now about a hundred feet out into the water.

We quickly threw everything into our bags and put our shoes back on. My stomach dropped as I realized that there was no clear solution to our situation. "Kathryn, I think we might be stuck."

Kathryn scrunched her eyebrows, biting her lip nervously. "Yeah ... this looks bad. What do we do?"

I fought back panic, trying to remain calm as I thought through our options. "Maybe we call for help." Another idea struck me. "Kathryn, how steep would you guess the beach is?"

Kathryn looked back at me, the fear in her voice changing to curiosity. "Pretty flat, I would guess. Why?"

I nodded, stroking my chin. "It might not be too deep out where we walked around that outcrop." I pointed to where the cliff stuck out into the ocean. Despite the even tone of my voice, I could feel fear within me as I watched the waves crash against the rocks. "If you don't mind getting wet, we could try to wade our way back to the stairs. Worst-case scenario, it's deep and we come back."

Kathryn looked hard at my face, trying to gauge my level of seriousness. I looked back at her, trying to maintain my cool. Kathryn nodded and swallowed hard. "Okay, but you're taller, so you should go first."

This seemed a reasonable request, and as a cold wind was whipping up, I was willing to pursue just about any option to get out of there sooner than with a rescue.

After we rolled our jeans up to the knees, I began wading out, following the edge of the cliff as I carefully plodded into deeper and deeper water. The sand, which had been firm when it was dry, now turned out to be more like mud soup, and before we were even twenty feet out it was threatening to steal our running shoes. Unfortunately, my overfilled backpack did not have room for the footwear, so Kathryn and I held our shoes in our hands. We also took this opportunity to roll our jeans as high above our knees as they would go, with the (unrealistic) hope of keeping them dry as we continued plodding forward.

By the time we got about halfway down the rocky outcrop, we were knee-deep in water. The violence of the aggressively rising tide had splashed seawater all over us, drenching our pants as well as our shirts. To make matters worse, the water was frigid, and the darkness had brought a cold wind that made this experience none too pleasant.

About this time, Kathryn spoke up. "Colin, I'm freezing." Her voice shook as she shivered.

"Me too," I noted, turning sideways as another wave came crashing in. "Do you want to turn back?"

The hesitation before the response was palpable. "No, I guess not."

We continued onward.

When we were twenty-five feet from the end of the promontory, I stepped forward and lost my footing. The water, which had been around waist-deep at this point, instantly jumped to shoulder-deep as I unwittingly stepped down a small ledge. I swung my arms, trying to maintain my balance, nearly dropping my shoes as I did. Drenched head to toe, I floundered back up to the shallower water.

Kathryn let out a slight yelp and offered me a hand. "Are you okay?"

I shook the water from my sopping sleeves. "Yeah, I'm not much wetter than before. It's deep. I don't think we can wade around this."

I looked up at the rocky outcrop, which flared out somewhat at the bottom. "We're pretty close to the end. It looks like we could climb up and shimmy along the last stretch above the water. That might be able to get us around."

Kathryn frowned, looking at the outcrop and then back to me. Her eyes seemed distant, her focus on shivering and not me. "Um, okay."

Using one hand for balance and the other to hold my shoes, I scrambled up the sharp rocks barefoot. I could hear Kathryn's soft footfall close behind, both of us wordless as we focused on the task at hand. We hugged the rock as we skirted around the edge of the cliff, picking our way along the uneven surface in the darkness. Fortunately, the waves did not reach us, and only the lightest sea foam stung my eyes as I strained against the darkness to find a path along the stone. Finally, after several minutes of scrambling, we reached the other side. The beach was mercifully higher here, allowing us to jump down into shin-deep water. I took a deep breath in relief. Only now did it dawn on me that, had either of us fallen near the deepest point, the water would have been over our heads. That, combined with our heavy clothing and bags, could have been a dangerous situation indeed.

Fortunately, on this side of the outcrop a walkable strip of dry sand led back to the stairs up the cliff. And as we reached the stairs, we were exuberant at our success and survival. But the walk back up the Torrey Pines trail to the cars was silent, quick, and cold. The seriousness of the risk we had just taken began setting in, probably right alongside hypothermia. Eventually, we did make it back, and after exchanging shivering high fives we made plans to meet up.

"See you at your place?" Kathryn inquired.

"Yeah! But first can we get food? I'm starving." I wrung my shirt as I spoke, splattering the pavement with seawater.

Kathryn smiled as she watched. "Okay! Where to?"

I continued twisting my clothes, water running down my hands as I spoke. "CYO Pizza! It's the best pizza place near my house."

Kathryn nodded. "Sounds good!"

I gave her the address, and soon we were both in our cars driving. With the heat blasting on full, I followed her out of the lot. When we reached the main road, she turned on her left blinker.

"Left? Is she mixed up? My house is right," I muttered to myself.

I turned on my right blinker, hoping she would notice. As traffic cleared, she made a left turn. Maybe Google had given her a weird route? Did she have the wrong address? My mind was abuzz with questions.

I decided it would be best to get to the freeway and give her a call from there. I turned right and started heading home. Only then did I realize that I had no idea where the heck I was going. I hurriedly opened Google maps—while simultaneously swerving around on the road—and eventually came to a face-palm-worthy realization: I was going the wrong way.

"No worries," I thought. "I can just make a U-turn and be back on track."

Annoyingly, it would be another two miles before I could make such a U-turn, and this delay had put me ten minutes behind Kathryn. Eager not to leave her waiting, I stepped on the gas and high-tailed it to the freeway.

In my rush, I hadn't considered the risks of going eighty-three miles per hour in a sixty-five zone. Fortunately, the cop who pulled me over was kind enough to spell them out for me. By the time the officer finished writing up a ticket, I was almost half an hour late, and Kathryn had already started texting to ask me where I was.

After sending a quick text explaining that I had been waylaid by the fuzz, I raced (at exactly the speed limit) over to the pizza place. When I showed up, my fresh ticket won me some serious pity points, which effectively nullified any bad PR I might have gotten from being horrifyingly late. After gorging ourselves on pizza, we headed back to my place, where a freshly made bed awaited us.

When we arrived, we raced up the two flights of stairs to my room. But once we got up the stairs and I saw my bed, I realized that it had been years since I had been with anyone other than Stella. The thought took hold and I struggled to maintain composure. It was the first time I had considered a romantic life without her, and I was having some serious second thoughts.

As soon as Kathryn entered the room, she shut and locked the door and had her clothes off before you could say, "Now hold on just a sec."

I continued standing in my room as still as the IKEA lamp across from me. Kathryn smiled, looking at me playfully. "Still dressed? What happened to all that excitement on the beach?"

For some reason, I couldn't stop thinking about the memories of sitting in bed with Stella, playing Boggle while enjoying a cup of French press coffee, or just talking with her while the sounds of Seattle rain came in through the bedroom window.

Kathryn was perceptive enough to notice something was off. "Something wrong?" She placed a hand on my back, her face one of genuine concern.

"No. It's nothing." I turned around and forced a smile. "You looking for excitement?" I picked her up and carried her to the bed as she giggled uncontrollably. I would not let my memories ruin our night.

But the choice to put the past behind me was not mine to make. Despite the great chemistry Kathryn and I had, I couldn't let go of the thoughts that had plagued me as I entered the room, and the experience left me confused and frustrated. I had been searching for someone exactly like Kathryn—why was I hesitating? Why could I not feel excited about this moment? Was it simply too soon? As we both lay on our backs in the dark, I could sense that something was off with her as well.

Kathryn's voice carried softly across the still of the room. "Colin, you said that you are quitting your job as a game designer."

I nodded, even though she couldn't see me. "That's right."

Kathryn shifted onto her side, and I turned my head toward her. I could only make out her silhouette, but there was no mistaking the concern in her tone.

She cleared her throat. "Where are you going next?"

I took a deep breath, rubbing the back of my neck and now staring at the ceiling. "I don't know. I won't stay in Carlsbad, I can tell you that."

Kathryn's tone was flat. "So, you're leaving San Diego."

I turned on my side to fully face her, still unable to make out anything in the dark of the room. "I didn't say that."

Kathryn's voice grew impatient. "But you're leaving Carlsbad, and your family and friends are all up in Seattle. It also has way more tech jobs. Why would you stay?"

I rolled onto my back and stared at the slowly blinking green light of the smoke detector directly above me. I hated that light. It kept me up every night with its incessant glow. I reached for it with my hand, as if being able to grab it would give me the answer. "I don't ... I don't know."

The room went quiet. I could hear cars passing by on the road outside. The wind whined through a crack in the bathroom window.

Kathryn rolled onto her side, facing away from me, so that we were no longer touching. Her breathing remained the same, not slow and steady like that of someone asleep. I tried to think of what to say, but no words came to mind.

The next morning Kathryn left. Despite our mutual affection, we agreed that it would probably be best not to keep seeing each other if I was going to be moving. But as brief as our time together was, my interaction with Kathryn marked a major turning point for me. As the days passed, I realized that I had made a huge mistake throwing away my previous life to be a game designer. My mad quest for professional glory had resulted in throwing out the baby, the bathwater, and the tub. What had started out as a life goal had become life-crushing. While I wasn't ready to admit that I had made a mistake, I began to recognize the things that had made me happy before. It was the moments in life that I spent playing Pokémon with Stella at Starbucks. It was the 3:00 a.m. trips to Taco Bell. I wanted to go back to that life.

Over the coming days, I resolved to call Stella and try to get back together. But before I picked up the phone, I thought long and hard about what I would say and how I would say it. My pitch needed to be perfect. I figured I only had one shot, so I didn't want to screw it up. I made flash cards. I practiced on my roommate.

By the time I finally pressed the green phone icon next to her name, I might as well have been ready to give the State of the Union address. I had intended the call to be a conversation, but from the moment she said hello my words came out as a speech. And as I spoke, she listened. She listened as I brought up the carefully artic-ulated points I had prepared about why we would be a great cou-ple. She listened as I reminisced about Pokémon and Taco Bell and discussions on the scientific progress of humanity. She listened as I took responsibility for moving to Seattle and focusing on my friends instead of her. She listened as I gushed about how much I loved her. At some point, I stopped talking, but she didn't stop listening.

"Stella ... ?" I asked tentatively.

"I'm still here, Colin." Her voice was soft and sad.

I could hear her inhaling and exhaling, but she wasn't speaking. I tried to keep a chipper tone. "So what do you say? Can we make it happen?"

A long silence passed. I didn't dare take a breath. "Stella?"

Her voice came through, weary. "I just ... I just don't think it's a good idea."

I sat back in my chair, stunned. My ears were ringing. The room spun. "So. So this is it. For good?"

You could hear the pause as Stella carefully formed her words. "No, I mean, I don't know. This break has been good for me. Like, really good. I ... I don't want to do long distance anymore."

I finally took in air. My ears perked and my tone lightened. "Are you saying that you would get back together if I moved up near Stanford?"

Stella let out a long-drawn-out sigh. "I don't know. Please don't move up here for me."

My heart felt heavy in my chest. "I see. All right. Well, thanks for listening to me. Bye, Stella."

"Bye, Colin."

When I hung up the phone, it felt like breaking up with her all over again. I was crushed, but I wasn't in tears. The room just kept spinning. I don't know if it ever stopped. As the days passed, I did the only thing I knew to do—I looked for a new job and kept going to work.

About a month after I called, I decided to drive up to San Jose, about thirty miles southeast of Stanford, to pay a visit to my uncle before the end of 2014. When I left Carlsbad, I had no intention of seeing Stella. After all, she had made it clear where she stood, and I didn't see any point in dragging out the matter further.

But while I was in the Bay Area, a friend of mine, Owen, invited me to a Stanford tailgate party, and I decided on a whim to go. I had only planned to stay for a weekend, and the game was on Sunday. I had a seven-hour drive back down to Carlsbad that same day, but since the party was in the morning, I could afford to spare a few hours.

Yet something felt odd as I drove onto campus. As I passed along Stanford's iconic Palm Drive, lined by vibrant flora and bustling students, my stomach tightened. I maneuvered into the lot where the cars were parked for the game, and I looked up at the looming eucalyptus trees that wooded it. Seeing the campus that I had walked so many times with Stella, which had so many memories tied to her, was almost too much. It felt like a baseball bat had hit me squarely in the chest.

I wanted to leave. Instead, I sat. I looked at the shadows of leaves on my dashboard and my arms. I watched the people excitedly hurrying by, sporting jerseys, flip-flops, and foam fingers. But most of all, I just looked at the tall eucalyptus trees, swaying gently in the wind. I picked up my phone and put my thumbs to work:

"Hey Stella, I'm in the area. Would you be interested in meeting me for a quick cup of coffee at Starbucks?"

I looked at the message long and hard. I looked back up at the trees. I hit "send."

The next two hours were the longest of my life. The tailgate party was a roller coaster of emotions. I could barely hold a conversation with any of the two dozen guests. Would she text me back? Would we see each other? Would I ever hear from her again? Was she angry?

" … And next thing you know the two of us were madly packing towels against the bathroom door to keep the water from flooding into the hallway, all while screaming for Andrew to let us in. What did you say again to get him to open the door, Colin?"

I snapped back into reality to see a group of smiling tailgaters looking at me, Owen expectant for a response. "Colin? You with us, man?" He placed his hands to his mouth. "Psht. Earth to Colin. Do you copy?"

"Oh. Yeah. Sorry." I stirred my mixed drink nervously as the partygoers exchanged amused glances. "Yeah, I uh ... don't recall."

Owen cleared his throat and continued. "Anyway, apparently Colin talked him into opening the door and ... "

My pocket vibrated. I pulled out my phone, a single text from Stella illuminating the dark screen:

"Okay."

After a few more back-and-forth messages, we decided that we would meet at her place and walk over; after all, the sun was shining brightly and the Starbucks wasn't far. I parked my car in front of her house. I rang her doorbell. I reminded myself to breathe. The door opened.

Stella stood before me, her face one of nervous excitement. "Hi, Colin."

A smile swept across my face. "Hi, Stella."

We exchanged hugs.

The conversation started out stiffly as we began walking the half mile to Starbucks. We talked about the weather—it was unseasonably warm, even for California—and about various current events. But by the time we reached our destination, things had jumped from forced and awkward to roaring along, just like the old days.

" ... You remember Professor May from my department here at Stanford, right?" Stella's eyes were alight as we sipped our iced lattes, her grin wry.

"Yeah, the super-old dude who never stopped talking?" I grinned back. Her smile was contagious.

"Yeah, that's the one. Our group's new first-year had no idea he would just keep going until you stopped him. He got stuck in a conversation for like two hours! The poor guy had no idea what to do."

I laughed deeply, riposting with a tale of my own. Before we knew it, the sun had set and the Starbucks was closing for the night. We walked back to her place.

"You want to come in for tea?" Stella asked, somewhat sheepishly.

My heart skipped a beat at the invitation. "Sure."

As we stepped inside, we found her roommates drinking wine downstairs, so she invited me up to her room where we could talk more privately. We sat on her bed, our voices low as she shared gossip on her roommates' lives. At some point, our hands brushed, and they stopped. Our eyes met as we fell silent.

"So," I said.

She looked to the side, somewhat uncomfortably. "Is this a good idea?"

My heart was racing, my mind unable to think. "You know how I feel. Only you can answer that question."

She half smiled, turning to the side. "Yeah but ... "

"But what?" I asked, my heart pounding through my chest.

Stella turned around. "Well, I could really use a back rub."

So I gave her a back rub. And as I did, she turned around and we kissed. It was a passionate kiss, one that only comes after months of waiting. We stopped after but a few seconds, but just so she could turn around to more fully embrace me. The intensity increased, and soon we could hardly tear each other's clothes off fast enough. I never drove home to Carlsbad that night.

The next morning found us in a difficult position. I asked her point blank if she wanted to get back together or not, and she remained firm that she didn't want to do long distance. Our solution was that if I could find a job in Silicon Valley, we would start dating for real again. Of course, this left us in a rather distressing dating-not-dating state, one I would not recommend to my worst enemy. To make matters even worse, we resolved it in the least productive way possible: with secrecy. From December 2014 until I eventually moved to Silicon Valley in late March of 2015, our relations were public to no one. After all, we weren't *officially* dating.

During this time, I frantically applied for jobs near her. This was partly to show my earnest desire to rekindle our love and partly to get the hell away from Rockstar. I'd given up on staying in the games industry, and I was searching for employment as just a run-of-the-mill software engineer. This made my employment prospects orders of magnitude better—the recruiter calls were rolling in faster than I could field them. After interviewing and receiving offers from several tech companies, I eventually decided on Facebook's newly acquired Oculus Virtual Reality division. It wasn't games, but it was damned exciting. I would be making virtual reality a real thing! I was so excited that I didn't even care if that made sense. I packed my bags for the second time in five months, and before you could blink, I was living just a few miles down the road from Stella. I had a dream job, a dream girl, and I lived in a wonderland of technology. I had finally made it.

Super Herpes

EFORE WE GO ANY FURTHER, I want you to know that you have my full permission to laugh at the suffering and misfortune that is about to follow. I say this because I suspect there is going to be a moment where you say, "Oh my god, why is he sharing this? Is he *insane*?" Of course, the answer is yes. But insane or not, if you are still game to see me burn my last shreds of dignity, sit back, buckle up, and get ready: this is going to be a bumpy ride. (Get it? 'Cause herpes is bumpy ...)

My first month after moving to Silicon Valley was glorious. I was back to making real money, and I was drowning in the Kool-Aid of being at the global hub of technology. Everyone I met was an overly analytic software engineer, just like me. Better yet, I only had to work five days a week, so I had plenty of time to hang out with Stella and my friends. And to add even more whipped cream and chocolate sauce to this delicious sundae that was my life, those friends were incredibly numerous, since so many of my college major class-mates had also ended up in Silicon Valley.

However, as picture perfect as this seems, things with Stella were slow to start. We only saw each other once or twice a week, mostly because Stella had a lot of work as a grad student. But I was not stressed. I figured that with enough time we would hit our stride. I was willing to be patient. This time, I wasn't going to screw it up.

I think it's about time we introduce this chapter's main character. Enter stage right: Mindy. Mindy was a red-haired, Irish American software analyst in the Messenger division of Facebook. She was short, although not really by female standards, and extremely fashionably pastel (all neon, all designer). We met at Mobile Karma, the now-nonexistent IT help desk for phone-related issues at Facebook. As a mobile engineer at Oculus, I needed a lot of Android phones, so I found myself there quite frequently. Since she also worked primarily with mobile devices, we bumped into each other a few times in line. On each of my visits, I would pull out my iPhone and play Hearthstone while waiting. A Hearthstone player herself, she would often comment on my performance over my shoulder. We became Facebook friends.

Now, you might be thinking, "Uh-oh, I see where this is going." But when Mindy and I first met, Stella was at the center of my world, and I was not the kind of guy to mess with a good thing. Then again, just how good of a thing did I have going? You may have noticed that my feelings toward Stella were, shall we say, pointedly asymmetric. In fact, at no point was she nearly as jazzed as I was to be restarting things.

Now, I want to dispense you some life advice, dear reader: If you are ever in a relationship where you and your significant other have this kind of mismatch, you probably shouldn't be in that relationship! I know, I know, you want it to work out. I did too. But trust me, it won't.

So it probably comes as no surprise to you that on June 21, 2015, at 4:13 p.m., about two months after I had moved from Carlsbad to Silicon Valley, Stella did what I saw as the unthinkable. She dumped me. And as she delivered the verdict, my world came crashing down. I cried. I begged. I pleaded. I did all the things you shouldn't do and generally acted like a three-year-old. I think "mutual" might be the perfect antonym for this breakup. As my roommates loved to put it at the time, I was a hot mess.

As an interesting aside, I think most people remember the day of their breakup as dark, gloomy, and raining. That kind of weather helps set the tone. However, if you aren't familiar with Stanford in June, it's nothing short of perfect. A typical day is seventy degrees with a cool breeze, and the soft smells of trees and flowers perfume the air. This day was no exception. Much like the day we got back together, it was spectacularly gorgeous, an ideal afternoon for sipping on an iced vanilla latte at Starbucks. (What can I say? I'm unashamedly basic.)

Regardless of how flawless the weather may have been, the next day, a Monday, I went to work a wreck. I was crying at my desk. I was totally unable to hold a conversation. Two new people started on my team that day, and when they met me I was Doom and Gloom. As far as first impressions go, I made one of the worst.

Yet, by a stroke of coincidence, on that very same Monday, Mindy decided to ask me to lunch. Somehow I managed to keep it together well enough for us to have a pleasant meal and conversation outside of the Sweet Stop, a hybrid bakery and ice cream parlor on Facebook's campus. We talked about Hearthstone, sci-fi, guitar, and music in general. She was very sweet, and a little shy at first, but

I felt like we hit it off. Later that day I invited her to come over to my house on Friday for a movie.

You might be thinking at this point that I had moved on remarkably quickly from my supposedly devastating breakup. To clarify that point, I should note that I spent most of the next several weeks when I wasn't at work lying on my back watching the ceiling fan spin. I would do this for several hours straight, without getting up for water, food, or anything. I didn't eat much, and my roommates, a couple of girls whom I'd gone to college with by the names of Marion and Vicky, grew seriously concerned for my well-being. So concerned, in fact, that they started coming up with creative solutions, such as writing encouraging messages on boxes of Triscuit (does anyone actually like that stuff?) and placing them in my room in the hopes I would eat them. It was a wonderful start to the summer. I wish I could tell you what I was thinking when I asked Mindy to come over for a movie that Friday, but for the life of me I couldn't. Given how hung up I was on the breakup and how emotionally wrecked I was, I can only speculate that this is pretty much the canonical definition of the word "rebound."

Eventually Friday came around, and we settled on *Moon,* a dark, slow-paced sci-fi thinkin' movie. It's not exactly romantic, but it was one of my favorites and a must-see for any fan of the genre. The movie went well enough, and we had gotten all cuddly on the couch under my faux leopard-skin blanket. A drained bottle of white wine sat empty on the floor, and the two of us were feeling positively bubbly. I went to put my arm around her, but then things got serious.

Mindy scooted away on the couch and turned to face me. She looked concerned, almost guilty. "Look, there's something I need to tell you, Colin." She wasn't smiling anymore.

I turned to face her, putting my arm down. My previously chipper smile vanished. "Uh-oh, what is it? Not feeling it? That's totally fine. I'm sorry if that was too rushed ... "

Mindy shook her head. "No, no, no. That's not it."

I raised an eyebrow and tilted my head slightly. "Then what is it?"

Mindy lifted her hands up in exasperation, shaking them slightly to emphasize that she didn't have a clear handle on the situation. "I have a boyfriend."

I slumped a little in my seat, looking down at the blanket that rested crumpled in my lap. "Ah. I see."

Mindy continued, now looking frustratingly off at the lifeless TV on which we had watched the movie. "And to be perfectly honest, I just ... "

I looked at her eyes, unclear where she was going with this. "Just what?"

Mindy made eye contact and flopped her arms on her lap in front of her. "I just wanted to fuck."

I stared back for a moment before responding. I can only imagine that my mouth was hanging open. "Oh."

I continued staring in disbelief. I think I was supposed to feel excited, or conflicted since she had a boyfriend, but I was just stunned. My brain crashed and rebooted, and I stumbled out some words.

"Well. Yeah. All right then."

Mindy pulled back a bit, raising an eyebrow and inflecting her voice. "What? You're cool with that?"

I rubbed the back of my neck, nodding slightly. The excitement I was supposed to feel was coming on now, but I was still too surprised to respond in any kind of coherent manner.

"Uh, totally. For sure."

Let's time-out for a second. I know how this looks. And honestly, I don't have anything to say in my defense. To be perfectly clear, I wasn't sure if she was in an open relationship or not. In fact, it's entirely plausible that she was cautioning that I shouldn't be interested in being exclusive. But I also didn't bother to clarify that point, which is not something that I'm particularly proud of. Nor am I proud of the fact that I am evidently the kind of person who would enable someone to cheat on their boyfriend. But that's what happened.

Upon my agreement, we both stood up and walked to my room. I was feeling uneasy about the whole boyfriend thing, but I tried to play it cool like it didn't bother me. I was also still feeling ridiculously emotional from my breakup just five days earlier. And yet somehow things just kind of went smoothly. I can imagine a million ways where this could have blown up, but it simply didn't. (In the interest of full disclosure, I told her that the breakup had happened a few weeks, not a few days, earlier. I don't know why I lied to her about that.)

I won't go into the gory details of how the next three hours went, but I think it's safe to say it was the best three hours of my life. You might be thinking, "MY GOD THAT IS A LONG TIME. THAT SOUNDS PAINFUL, ESPECIALLY FOR HER." And yeah, toward the end it was getting there. For the record, I recommend AstroGlide X as my personal lubricant of choice. I wasn't paid to say this or anything. (Note to editor: follow up with AstroGlide and see if they will pay me to say this.) It's just something that I have found works well for my needs. It's nice because its silicone-based, so it's hydrophobic (meaning it works fantastically in showers and tubs), and it doesn't have glycerin so it won't cause yeast infections. It also is latex-safe, which is an obviously important point. One major caveat is that you shouldn't use it with anything else silicone-based (*cough* Lelo) so keep that in mind. (On second thought, maybe I should have named this book "Adventures in Silicone Valley.")

Anyway, the main reason why our sexcapades took so long is that ... well ... condoms feel ... weird. I mean it's just not natural (trigger warning: *really* stupid decision incoming). So, after about two hours of not being able to finish, Mindy stopped me. At this point we were both covered with sweat and thoroughly exhausted.

Mindy placed a hand on my shoulder. "Look, I can tell this isn't working ... Do you just want to take it off?" Her face was compassionate, showing sympathy, not frustration.

I looked at her, my eyes widening in alarm. "The condom?"

Mindy nodded. "Yeah." Her voice remained even and cool, the gentlest of smiles on her face.

I sat up straight, making full eye contact. My face was serious. "Isn't that kind of risky? I mean, I don't have any STDs, but you don't know that. Do you have any?"

Mindy shook her head, remaining calm. "No. I don't think so, at least."

I rubbed my chin, mulling over the idea. "You're on birth control?"

Mindy shook her head again. "No, but I had a boyfriend who I did this with a lot before, and I just ended up making a lot of trips to the local pharmacy for Plan B."

I stared at her dumbfounded. "Isn't that like ... really expensive? Also, I hear that stuff is just horrible to use."

Mindy shrugged. "Yeah, I mean, it's definitely not an ideal solution."

I stared at her for a moment. For the second time tonight, I couldn't believe what I was hearing. Her complete comfort with such a risky proposition was throwing me for a loop. And once more my brain checked out on me, leaving me to figure things out for myself.

And while we're here, let me dispense some more valuable life advice: Don't make important decisions (such as those regarding birth control and protection usage) DURING SEX. There are some powerful hormones at play and they might fog your judgment ever so slightly. Given this disclaimer, I think it's clear what happened next: the condom came off and we finished.

Afterwards, we sallied on out to the nearest Walgreens to pick up some Plan B. I think we were both in good spirits despite that trip, which likely turned some heads as we were still quite sweaty and our hair was absolutely a mess. When we got back to my place, Mindy had another surprise in store for me: she promptly had to return home to her boyfriend. And while that probably should have been a bit of a downer, I remained in reasonably good spirits.

Looking back at this situation, it's not exactly the smartest move to have unprotected sex with someone who is clearly seeing other people. In fact, looking forward I would have probably said the same thing. Probably at literally any point in time I would have said that what I did was an exceptionally bad idea, except evidently during sex. The birth control issue is just icing on that towering cake of risky decision-making. And while it is something that I hope I would never do again—and that I view as the result of a set of circumstances that were highly favorable to this outcome—it scares me to think that I am capable of something as stupid as that.

Despite all of this, Mindy and my casual relationship proceeded through the coming weeks, but with the added benefit of proper birth control. By this juncture, I had figured out that her existing relationship wasn't open, and I was racked with guilt. Naturally, I turned to the nearest people I could trust for advice: my roommates.

To the great shock of, well, no one, they were pointedly against our continued involvement, which in hindsight gave Mindy and I seeing each other a kind of forbidden-fruit appeal. And thus, despite my roommates' repeated requests, pleas, and every manner of begging to cease and desist (which mostly revolved around fears that I would end up killed by the boyfriend with a pipe wrench in the living room, leaving them to deal with the mess), Mindy and I continued seeing each other.

Given my prior talk of not being into hookups and wanting to return to a stable relationship, you might wonder why I continued to see her. Well, I think most people would guess it was the amazing sex. But I want to posit an alternative explanation (you can start rolling your eyes now). When I look back on what compelled me to continue, I think the main thing was that she seemed genuinely kind and affectionate. I liked her a lot, and as she explained it, her continuing relationship with her boyfriend was more a financial necessity (they lived together) than an emotional one. And I was empathetic to this position. I mean, here you have someone who doesn't make a lot of money by California Bay Area standards, where rent for a *shared room* can be around $1,500 a month, and she's stuck continuing to date this guy simply because they have a reasonably priced and rent-controlled place. That sucks!

To summarize, my mental model of the situation was basically this: Mindy was a fundamentally faithful person who was in a bad place money-wise, largely due to the wildly high cost of living. I had a hunch that she and her boyfriend had an "understanding"; they were only nominally together and were both seeing other people. And when I frame it that way, it sounds a lot less scandalous, now, doesn't it? I told you I wasn't a bad person! (Wait, I didn't say that? I said that I *was* a bad person? Oh. Well yeah, I guess that's probably true, too.)

Unfortunately, this narrative has a few holes. The first was that Mindy kept posting gushing and oh-so-adoring Instagram para-graphics about how much she loved her boyfriend. On top of that, she encouraged me to date other people, since we weren't exactly an exclusive couple. I was initially resistant to this idea, mostly because I eventually wanted to be in an exclusive relationship with her. I said as much, but she was not shy about reminding me of my place as her fling. My second-place position in her life stung me emotion-ally, and my interests slowly began to diversify.

Despite what appears to be a rumbling volcano on the verge of eruption (in bed?), this situation did not end catastrophically. Rather, it continued for several months, in a seemingly stable man-ner. Mindy and I went on dates to some amazing places, such as the Legion of Honor and the Taco Bell on Pacifica Beach (which is more like "UH-MAZING!" than amazing). Things were, dare I say it, chugging along quite well. But as the clocks rolled over to the New Year of 2016, my fortunes were about to change.

One day, Mindy seemed decidedly troubled on a visit to my house. As soon as she arrived, she sat down on the couch and looked out the window with a frown on her face. I was slow to catch on; likely I was fetching a can of Mountain Dew from the kitchen. But as I stepped into the living room, I noticed her distanced gaze.

I sat down next to her, placing a hand on her shoulder. "Hey, Mindy, what's going on?" Being comforting has never been a strong skill of mine, but I did my best to muster it.

Mindy shrugged, but didn't say anything or change her fixed stare.

I pressed further, moving between her and the window. "Something is wrong. Talk to me."

Mindy shook her head and returned my concerned look with a blank expression. "It's nothing."

I pressed onward. "I can tell it's not nothing."

Mindy finally broke and pulled out her phone. A minute later she held it up and showed me my OkCupid dating profile, showing recent activity. "What is this all about?"

I furrowed my brow and straightened up my posture. "I don't understand. I thought you wanted me to see other people."

Mindy returned to looking out the window. "But you said you only wanted to see me."

I squinted my eyes and folded my arms. "Yeah, but that was kind of predicated on the fact that you wouldn't continue living with your boyfriend. Where do you come off getting on my case about this?"

Mindy looked at me again, her volume rising only slightly. "I told you why I was still with him. It's not like we're doing anything."

I rolled my eyes. "Except going to bed together every night."

Mindy glared back at me.

I met her gaze with a neutral but earnest expression. "All right, I hear you. I'll stop when you stop posting gushing love letters to him on your news feed."

Mindy turned away from me sharply. "Yeah, whatever."

Sadly, we were never able to reach an agreement on this, which only strained things further.

A few days later, another issue cropped up that was much more ... pointed. On the morning of January 6, 2016, I woke up to what can only be described as the most alarming situation I have ever encountered in my life. In the span of that evening, my nether regions had gone from normal to *thoroughly* covered in small red blisters. I had an STD.

You might be thinking to yourself, "Colin, how did you NOT think this was going to happen? ISN'T IT OBVIOUS, GIVEN YOUR CHOICES?" To which I say, "Um, yeah, in hindsight that does seem pretty obvious, doesn't it?" Feel free to be baffled at my cluelessness. I certainly am.

But on this morning, I did not have time to be self-critical, because I was panicking. Borderline in tears, I called my doctor immediately and requested an appointment PRONTO. The receptionist, a very polite young man, informed me that the soonest my doctor could see me would be next week. NEXT. WEEK. Nuh-uh, no way that was going to work. This needed attention now.

I started dialing every doctor, walk-in clinic, and person wearing a lab coat or stethoscope I could get ahold of. After a few frantic calls, I reached an Urgent Care clinic in nearby Foster City that could see me that night. I accepted this appointment, deciding that I could at least wait half a day since this wasn't quite worth a trip to the ER (I had been there two months prior for salmonella and was not particularly keen to make a second visit). As soon as I hung up the phone, I steeled myself to pass one of the most painfully slow days of my life.

In case you ever have an unknown STD and can't see a doctor until that evening, I highly recommend taking the day off work. I didn't, and that certainly was a mistake. Aside from the stress of the situation, which made it nigh impossible to focus, the powerful urge to find out what was going on was driving me insane. As you might imagine, Google Image searching "What STD do I have?" while cross-referencing with symptoms was not exactly an option at work. (By the way, through this process of identification I have seen things that can never be unseen.)

However, after a few trips to a bathroom stall, I concluded that herpes was the only reasonably likely candidate for my condition. I was devastated, but not entirely surprised. Eventually, my appointment time came up and I made the solemn drive to the doctor.

As I stepped through the doors of the doctor's office, it felt like walking to an execution. To everyone around you, this is a normal day. The receptionist looked bored, the other people looked all kinds of normal sick—nothing too extraordinary. But I walked as a dead man, awaiting the delivery of my sentence.

When I stepped up to the reception counter, I was mercifully not asked why I was seeing the doctor. (I probably would have coolly said, "I GOT THE HERPES AND I'M FREAKING OUT!") Instead, the receptionist handed me a form where I could explain my problem. I wrote plainly, "I definitely have an STD. Pretty sure it's herpes." I handed the form back and found a seat.

It felt like an eternity passed before I was led into an examination room. When a nurse finally took me back, I plopped down on the bench and sat to await my fate. The nurse took my vitals, but didn't ask any questions (I can only imagine she read the sheet and didn't exactly feel like prying). After what felt like a second eternity, the doctor finally came in. He was old, short, and very hairy, but he had a quick way of speaking and an outgoing demeanor.

"All right, so you think you have herpes?" He looked down at a clipboard, chuckling. "Don't worry, there are probably a hundred different things it could be, and herpes is not the most likely. Let's take a look. It's probably going to be something curable."

His calm, confident, and friendly manner assuaged my fears. Had I been freaking out over nothing? How silly of me. I was such a silly goose. In any case, I took off my pants.

Within a mere second, the doctor responded, "Oh. I see."

An awkward silence passed.

He took a closer look, and his face went from confidently reassuring to somewhat uncomfortable. "Well, uh, yeah. That's definitely herpes."

I gasped audibly and met his eyes with a look of cold sadness. "Oh."

His lips tensed up and he looked at me blankly. "Yep."

I put my pants back on and tried my best to not look like I was panicking. But I was panicking. My life was over. How could I have not seen this happening. Stupid, stupid, Colin.

I choked out some words. "Are you ... sure?"

The doctor picked up his clipboard and fidgeted with a pen, avoiding eye contact. "Well, I am not really sure what else it could be ... That does look like herpes. I mean, it could be a yeast infection, but that would be pretty unlikely."

The axe came down and my head rolled. I could feel the color draining from my face. It was over.

My voice barely managed a hoarse whisper. "So, what now, Doctor?"

The doctor took a seat and did his best to keep his voice even and calm. "Well, I am guessing you spent most of today reading about this, and if you didn't then you probably will tonight. You're going to be more of an expert than me in short order." He chuckled slightly. "In any case, you know the drill: it's with you for life, you can spread it even when you don't have symptoms, and you need to talk to partners *before* having sex." He put some emphasis on that last point and looked me straight in the eye.

I nodded. After some follow-up Q and A, he pulled out his Rx pad and wrote me a prescription for valacyclovir.

Clearing his throat, he handed me the slip of paper. "Fortunately, you came in at the start of the first outbreak, which means that if you take the valacyclovir, you might never get another one. It should clear up soon."

I took my prescription slip, walked outside, and got into my car. At least this time it was raining, and fittingly so. I felt completely numb. I picked up the phone and did the only thing I knew I had to do: I called Mindy.

My voice was shaking as she picked up the phone. "Hi, Mindy."

Mindy didn't notice and sounded cheerful at the unexpected call. "Hi, Colin. What's up?"

I spoke slowly at first, gradually increasing in volume and intensity as my panic level rose. "Well, I just got back from the doctor and he says I have herpes. Do you have herpes? Do you know if you have herpes? You might have it and not know it. You should definitely get tested, though, and we probably shouldn't do anything until we get this straightened out."

There was a pause, followed by a very concerned reply. "No, I don't have herpes. I'll get tested right away."

I waited for her to lash out, to be angry, to scold me, to say *something*, but nothing followed. I swallowed, closing my eyes as I listened for words that never came. Finally, I spoke. "So, what does this mean for us?"

I knew her well enough to know that silence meant trouble, but not well enough to know exactly what kind. Eventually, she sighed. "I don't know. Let's talk about this in person after I get tested."

I nodded, though she couldn't see. "Yeah, all right."

"I'll talk to you later, Colin."

"Bye."

"Bye."

Mindy took a blood test the next morning and it came back negative a few days after that. This did not look good for me.

In the following week, I took the medication as prescribed. My primary care doctor dragged me in to "see for herself," as she had become somewhat skeptical of my ailments due to their recent variety and number (salmonella, shoulder surgery, sinus infection, etc.). Encouraged by her honeyed words that I was probably misdiagnosed and that it was likely something else, I went into her office to get a second opinion. She gave me a blood test that included everything and the kitchen sink, and I came back clean on everything, including herpes (and kitchen sinks). Unfortunately, the herpes test is not diagnostic so early on into contracting the virus, and realistically I probably still had it. Her visual diagnosis suggested as much as well, although she noted that there were other, less likely, possibilities. I would need to wait six months and get blood-tested again to be 100% sure.

After a week, I finished the valacyclovir. However, the symptoms were not alleviated. Quite to the contrary, the tiny red bumps were marching down my thighs and up toward my belly button. My level of concern rose from miserable acceptance to crisis-level stress. My only consolation was that herpes could take three weeks to clear, so I figured this must be par for the course. Surely this was just a part of the recovery process ... Right?

Unfortunately, Mindy was growing increasingly impatient. In an act of maturity and kindness, she had promised not to stop seeing me because of the diagnosis. However, since she had turned up negative, she was becoming less and less receptive to my inability to explain the situation. (To be fair, Mindy was the only person I had been sleeping with, so it legitimately was a conundrum to me as well. Truly the truth is stranger than fiction.) At around the two-week mark, I stopped hearing from her altogether.

By two and a half weeks, the symptoms were still going strong. Rather, I should say *growing* strong, because they continued to spread down my legs and up my torso unabated. Naturally, I scheduled a follow-up appointment with my primary care doctor. After taking another look, she gave me a second dose of valacyclovir and told me that if it still hadn't cleared in a week I would need to see a dermatologist.

By this point I was freaking out. Scratch that. I was FREAK-ING THE FUCK OUT. I had been scouring forums, websites, medical textbooks, and anything I could get my hands on for the better part of January trying to figure out how to deal with this. I had a dozen pamphlets with titles like *Living with Herpes* strewn around my room. I was not a happy camper.

As the three-week mark passed, I returned to full-blown panic mode. By this point I was an expert on herpes. I could tell you how common it was in what countries, what percentage of people knew they had it, and all the methods of diagnosis. (For the record, one-sixth of the population has it in the USA, with only about 10–20% of those people knowing they have it. This figure blew my mind; I had no idea it was so common. If we assume that my readership is a representative sample, then around 4% of people reading this both have herpes and know they have it. (I'm sorry, guys. I feel your pain :(.)

My reading also turned up a distressing possible explanation for why my herpes outbreak wouldn't go away. I learned that for some people with compromised immune systems, like those with AIDS, the herpes symptoms either would remain indefinitely or would come back very frequently. And for some of these people, nothing was wrong with their immune system; it just couldn't deal with herpes. Among the people who had herpes and knew they had it, the percentage who also had these persistent symptoms due to derpy immune systems was small (IIRC <5%), and they usually required suppressive antiviral drug therapy. I dubbed this group "Super Herpes" people, even though the virus was the same and it was just their immune systems that weren't dealing with it. From what I could tell, these people were getting the short end of an already very short stick.

Despite their small numbers, the people with Super Herpes were a particularly vocal group on the forums. Many people spoke of lives of abstinence to spare the world their suffering. One man stated that—and I'm paraphrasing because I couldn't find the exact post again—"I thought I had it bad when I got HIV. But let me tell you, this herpes thing has been WAY WORSE. Painful blisters all day, every day. I had no idea things could get this bad." If normal herpes, at its longest and untreated, took three weeks to clear, then how was I, at three and a half weeks, anything but certain to have Super Herpes?

At four weeks, I finished the second round of valacyclovir. The symptoms were still at peak levels; the drugs might as well have been a placebo. I called the dermatologist to make an appointment.

By now I had fully resigned myself to my fate. I was all but donning brown monk robes and shaving my head. A life of chastity lay ahead of me—but you know what, it wasn't going to be that bad. I mean, it wasn't like my dating prospects on the West Coast were that great to begin with, right? One less thing on my plate? I would get through this. I would survive. I would imbue my life with new meaning.

Finally, the day of the dermatology appointment came. The dermatologist had been clued in by my primary care doctor as to what was going on, and I can only assume she was preparing to bring on the "big guns" reserved for those with immune systems that just didn't know what to do.

When she walked into the room, I think "serious" would be the best way to describe the atmosphere. There was no consoling, no words of encouragement. We both knew that that time had passed. After a standard full skin exam, she looked down under.

Her face lit up immediately. "I have some great news for you, Colin."

I looked at her, my desolate expression improving only marginally. "What?"

She beamed back at me. "You don't have herpes."

If I hadn't been sitting in my birthday suit (save for a paper gown), I would have jumped for joy. My eyes shot fireworks and a grin the size of Montana swept across my face. "What! YES! THIS IS GREAT! Wait, what *do* I have?" I screwed up my face in mixed fear and excitement, uncertain which emotion to portray and failing decidedly at both.

The doctor took a seat, placing her hands together. "Molluscum. Meaning not permanent. It's quite common in children. They mostly get it from roughhousing in pools or sharing towels, but it's rare in adults. It can be quite intense when adults do get it, and it's very frequently misdiagnosed as herpes."

I nodded, trying to listen earnestly without looking too delighted. "Oh, I see. So, what happens now?"

The doctor looked down at the floor, making a wide gesture with her hands. Her face remained solemn despite having given me a new lease on life. "Well, if left untreated it can take years to go away. And it's very contagious."

I let out a sigh, the color draining from my face once more. "Great. Out of the pan and into the fire. I trade one horrible disease for another. But wait, how long does it take to go away with treatment?"

She looked up at me, but didn't smile. "Usually about a month. Could be a few."

My expression returned to pure delight; my enormous grin returned. "Sign me up! What do we have to do?"

Her serious expression remained. "Well, I am going to have to treat the affected area with..." (Wait for it) "... liquid nitrogen."

For those who do not know what liquid nitrogen is or why this is something that you should be alarmed at, it's nothing shy of the most excruciating medical procedure I have ever experienced. As a child, I had many warts on my feet removed through this method, which usually resulted in me screaming at the top of my lungs. (It feels like someone is stabbing you with a fiery needle.)

How this works is the doctor starts with a bottle of liquid nitrogen, which sits at a cool −321°F. The doctor then uses either a sprayer or a dabber to apply the frigid substance to a patient. Being so ungodly cold, it freezes anything it touches immediately on contact, which does nothing to treat skin viruses. However, having a chunk of flesh flash-frozen is so alarming to the body that it causes an intense local immune system reaction, which typically eliminates any viruses in the area. Usually this procedure is used to treat warts and other benign viral skin conditions, like molluscum, which your immune system would otherwise take a pass on because it's a lazy bum about fighting these kinds of things.

Immediately after hearing the proposed treatment, and given that I was familiar with the experience, you might imagine that the look on my face right now was one of horror at the idea of having a VERY painful procedure applied to a VERY sensitive region. But no sirree, I was grinning like an idiot. This was the best news I had ever gotten. Of course, the actual application of the liquid nitrogen was excruciating. As the icy fire had its way with me, it was all I could do to keep from yelling and recoiling from the unbearable pain (I did a lot of recoiling, despite my best efforts). I imagine that if someone had walked in and seen the doctor applying the cold liquid, and seen me smiling ear to ear while flinching, they would have believed I was a true masochist.

As soon as I left, I texted Mindy the good news—mostly to give her some peace of mind. I didn't get a reply, but what I did get was a new understanding. Excuse me a moment while I step onto this stump.

Rewinding a bit, a couple weeks after my initial misdiagnosis, I went to a company holiday party where I had a double-blind date set up for me and another coworker, Marco. (To be clear, this was two blind dates, not double-blind as in the person setting us up didn't know who was getting what. That does kind of sound fun, though!) During the event, the four of us hung out and generally had a very nice time. However, at one point in the evening, Marco made a good-natured dirty remark, with the follow-up being, "I mean, it's not like I have herpes!"

I tell you, when I heard that, I felt about this small: →←. What's worse is that I probably could have been the one making that joke just a month prior. It's so hard to know who your audience is when you make an offhand remark like that.

As I said earlier, by most estimates, one in six people in the USA have herpes. It's a staggering number, and something that NO ONE talks about. Before I got molluscum, if you had asked me to guess how many people I knew with herpes, I would have said zero. Now, I am sure I know several people, but have they ever said anything about it? No, they haven't. The stigma is insanely large, and largely undeserved given how common it is and how minor the symptoms are for the majority of people. And as I mentioned before, in no fewer than 80% of cases, the symptoms are so minor that people don't even know they have it. Thinking I had it for a month and a half did a lot to change my perspective on the matter, and while I am thankful that I do not have herpes, I gained a great deal of empathy for those who do.

As for Mindy, I never heard back. Despite a few texts assuring her that I was STD-free and that I had the documentation to prove it, she was gone for good. I didn't particularly feel like swinging by her desk or otherwise confronting her at work, and so, with a heavy heart, I ended up chalking the whole thing up as a loss and moving on.

What's in a Name, Anyway?

AFTER EVERYTHING THAT HAPPENED, it probably comes as no surprise that things ended the way they did with Mindy. At the time, it seemed like such a shame, but then again, at least I didn't get killed by her boyfriend with a pipe wrench (or need to flee to Bolivia).

However, during the second half of 2015, my dating adventures were not confined to just seeing Mindy. Remember how she encouraged me to date other people? Let's take a closer look at that.

About two months into the Mindy fling, about mid-August of 2015, I set my attention once more to online dating. Having had a fair amount of experience in Seattle and San Diego, I was keen to put my learnings to use as I eyed Silicon Valley. My OkCupid profile was now a well-oiled machine; I had hundreds of women matching at over 90%. Every week I had edited and refined my written bio, and it read like a well-polished résumé. I now had guitar pics, hiking pics, and pics with dogs that I didn't even own. As a result, my ability to get first dates improved, and I began to wonder if I could broaden my reach.

To this end, I expanded beyond Tinder and OkCupid, adding the dating apps Hinge, Bumble, and Coffee Meets Bagel to my collection. Each app had its own pros and cons, and I applied the same methodologies to them as I had to OkCupid and Tinder. Slowly, my trickle of women turned into a stream.

Five dates a week became standard. I kept my weekends and evenings clear, scrapping all other plans to leave room for dating. And to manage the load, I resolved to stop planning each date on its own, opting for bubble tea shops as my go-to suggestion. It was the kind of place where you could hold a quiet conversation and a table for as long or as short as you wanted. And unlike coffee shops, for most people this was a new experience, so it counted as an interesting date for my partner. Plus, tea shops tended to be ultra-public locations, making safety less of a concern for my date. To boot, they usually kept generous hours, so they could handle any time slot. Undoubtedly, bubble tea was the perfect first date.

I took a weekend to find a suitable tea shop in every part of the San Francisco Bay Area. After gorging myself for fifty-eight hours on sugary, caffeinated drinks, I now had a map of a half-dozen locales. My date selection became incredibly simple. Meeting me on a Sunday afternoon in Redwood City? Cha Time. Catching an evening drink in Mountain View? Tea Era. Scootering on over to hit me up in San Francisco? Boba Guys. Looking for love in Oakland? Mr. Green Bubble. I had turned the process of searching for love into an assembly line, and I was cranking out dates as fast as one humanly could. (If you want to read some of my learnings from this online dating bender, check out Secret Bonus Chapter B.)

Yet as I dated more and more, I felt less and less. The routine made my dates mundane. In addition to going to the same places, I found that I was asking the same questions and sharing the same stories. I never felt a spark, even when others felt it for me. I started wondering if my rapid pace was making me distant and cold. To combat this, I made a rule to go on at least two dates with anyone who was willing, where the second date was something a little more thought-out, just to make sure I wasn't passing on someone I should seriously consider. I did very little other than date, eat, work, date, and sleep. Oh, and date. I did that too.

Yet no matter how many people I saw, no one was catching my eye. I churned through women, slowly losing faith in my highly optimized system as person after person failed to make a match. By now I had picked through all the ladies who wowed me, and I wasn't seeing people that excited me anymore. Fresh faces were becoming rare, and my interest in dating began to wane. As mid-October of 2015 approached, I finally decided to give up.

However, that didn't stop me from wistfully browsing through my dating profile from time to time. And one evening a couple of weeks after I had called it quits, I found a girl who, right from the get-go, distinguished herself from the pack. She did this by introducing herself to me in the most unlikely of ways: by messaging me on OkCupid.

Now, you might be cocking your head a bit, squinting your eyes, and wondering why that is so odd. After all, isn't the point of OkCupid for people to message each other? Why should it be so surprising that a cute girl messaged me?

I can't speak for people living outside of Silicon Valley, but for those who do live there, there is a fundamental truth that nearly everyone knows: Girls basically don't first-contact guys in online dating. In fact, the difference in first messages between the genders is staggering. To demonstrate this, I did a little experiment—I looked at my average received first messages per week and compared it to a sample female profile that I whipped up for science.

First, let's look at how mine fared. My profile had hundreds of questions filled out and a handful of people had read and critiqued the content. It's probably the most well-vetted thing I have ever submitted to the world. Additionally, I spent dozens of hours optimizing my questions using k-means clustering algorithms and data mining methods. Despite all this effort, I only got about one person per week who initiated contact with me. When I talked to my male friends, I found that I was doing considerably better than most of them—many had never received a first message since they'd started using OkCupid.

Now, let's look at the profile I made using a stock photo of a woman from the Internet. I picked someone not super hot, but passably attractive. Someone on the low to mid end of who I would click on. I named her Naomi and she was twenty-four, straight, fit, single, and lived in Redwood City—same as me, except for the female part. I only had the one photo, but whatever, that would have to do. I answered about a hundred basic questions for her in roughly the same way I would have for myself. The profile description was vague and generic—I think I just talked about hiking, travel, and Netflix. I put it up for a week.

At the end of that week, the results were staggering. My sample woman had 236 new messages. I could spend hours just reading through them. I was so surprised that I asked my female roommates at the time—Marion and Vicky—if their results were similar. It turned out that their numbers were *even higher.* When I considered how many handcrafted messages had been sent to this fake woman, most of which would never even be read and all of which were drawing dead, a little piece of me died.

While I would hardly describe this little experiment as scientific, it illustrates my point that men typically are the ones who do the reaching out. So naturally you can understand my surprise when I was messaged out of the blue by one of the most attractive people I have ever seen on OkCupid. She had long tan hair and sharp features. Her smile was genuinely warm, and her eyes seemed full of energy in every shot. Her delicate physique was carefully back-dropped in a variety of international locales. We had a 99% match, likely the product of my highly optimized approach to question answering, and her message was clear and to the point:

"Hey! Let's get dinner in SF sometime!"

Shortly after, she sent a second message:

"I mean, like, if you want ... I didn't mean to sound so command-ing."

By the time I saw these—a full three weeks after she penned them—I had completely stopped using OkCupid and was contemplating deleting the app. Why I even checked my messages on that day, I don't know. And as I read her missives, I was both horrified and delighted. My first reaction:

"Uh-oh, maybe she is another Amber and she won't look like her profile pics."

I looked carefully for signs of touch-up, odd lighting, or weird camera angles. Nothing seemed out of place. My next thought:

"Crap! What if she isn't single anymore? It's been two weeks!"

I figured I was pretty much doomed. I looked over her profile for other red flags, discovering that she played League of Legends, one of my favorite video games, and was a software engineer who minored in economics like myself. Was this a dream? Could such a woman exist and be reaching out to *me*?

No. I wouldn't believe it. Surely, she was a Nigerian princess who needed me to wire her money in exchange for riches. Or maybe her photos were expertly doctored. Or worst of all, maybe she was a catfish. (For those who don't know, a catfish is someone who pretends to be someone they are not using social media, usually with the intent of surreptitiously luring people into deceptive online romances.)

Despite every fiber of my body warning me that this was certainly a trap, I threw caution to the wind and hurriedly sent off a response.

"Heck yes, let's do it! Sorry I stopped checking this. If you are still down shoot me a text: XXX XXX XXXX."

Normally I tend to be a little coyer—I don't usually give out my phone number and outright express interest, but I didn't want to risk blowing her obvious interest in me. Much to my surprise, she texted me within seconds.

"Hi Colin. This is the OKC user you just gave your number to. My name is Nancy. When are you free to come up to SF for dinner?"

After some back-and-forth, we chose a restaurant named Umami Burger near the ballpark in downtown San Francisco as our meet-up location for the coming Friday.

On the day of our date, I realized that this restaurant was a particularly poor choice, as I had to drive up from Redwood City—a full forty-five minutes to the south in good traffic—and then find parking during a ball game. When I arrived, unsurprisingly there was no parking to be found. I did eventually find a spot two miles away, and caught a cab over to the restaurant. Fortunately, the powers that be were not decidedly capricious on this day, and the game was still going, so the burger place was nearly empty.

As I stepped through the front door, I took a quick glance around. I mostly expected to see a man dressed up to look sort of like the woman whose pictures I saw, or maybe a woman would be there but would turn out to have a hook for a hand, an eye patch, and a peg leg. As I looked for my date, thoughts of what horrible surprise surely must be in store filled my mind. I heard a female voice behind me. This was starting to feel eerily familiar.

"Hi, Colin!" the sweet sing-songy voice beckoned.

I turned around slowly, preparing myself for the worst. My expression must have been one of unchecked fear and anxiety. But much to my delight, before me stood a woman with long tan hair and sharp features. Her smile was genuinely warm, and her eyes seemed full of energy. Her delicate physique seemed perfectly back-dropped into the chic atmosphere of the restaurant, and as I realized that she was, in fact, the woman I had seen online, a broad smile overtook my face.

"Uh. Hi. Hi, Nancy," I stammered. I did a second scan for an Adam's apple or pirate-themed prosthetics: two eyes, two legs, two arms, both hands—yep, she checked out.

Nancy returned my smile and offered a hug, which I graciously accepted. The aroma of fresh flowers filled my nose—even her hair smelled nice!

She took a step back, tilting her head slightly as she spoke, her broad smile still there. "So, do you want to get a seat?"

I grinned so widely that I must have looked like a complete buffoon. If I was dreaming, I never wanted to wake up. "Yeah, let's um ... let's do that!"

The restaurant host had been watching this interaction, and a wry smirk revealed his understanding of my situation. He led us to a table for two near the back, where we sat down.

Nancy wasted no time in getting the conversation started. Her smile vanished and was replaced by a more inquisitive expression. "So, you went to Harvey Mudd College?"

I blinked, and my smile faded. "Uh, yeah. How did you know that? It's not on my profile."

Nancy smiled again, shrugging as she giggled slightly.

I narrowed my eyes, casting her a concerned glance. "Not going to explain that?"

She continued giggling. "I go to Claremont McKenna College."

I immediately relaxed. For those who don't know, Harvey Mudd College sits on the same campus as four other undergraduate colleges: Pitzer, Scripps, Claremont McKenna, and Pomona. The combined student body size is around five thousand, which means that it's quite common for students of different schools to know each other. Additionally, since students can take classes at any of the schools, it's possible we had even had a class together.

I smiled back at her. "Ah! So you knew me from school?"

She shook her head, still grinning. "Nope."

I gave her a somewhat confused look. "So how do you know where I went to college?"

She kept smiling and giggled once more. "So, what are you going to order?"

At this point I decided that she was probably just having some fun with me, and that we almost certainly had bumped into each other on campus. I changed the topic slightly. "If I am not mistaken, you said you are still a student at Claremont McKenna. Isn't school in session right now?"

Nancy nodded, grinning fiercely. "Yeah, duh."

My eyebrows shot to the top of my head. The Claremont Colleges sit on the eastern edge of Los Angeles County, and for those who aren't super familiar with California geography, we were at that exact moment 414 miles by car from the school she was supposedly attending, while school was in session.

I pressed further, trying to make sense of the apparent paradox. "Okay, so why are you here? Interviews?"

She continued her wicked grin and shook her head. "Nope!"

My face scrunched so hard it wore permanent lines into itself. "Are you going to explain any of this to me?"

She giggled once more. "I think I'm going to get the Umami burger with bacon."

I thought for a moment—what if she didn't go to Claremont McKenna? What if she was making everything up? What if this was another Amber! I needed a test. I could throw the names of some students her way and see if she knew them. Yes ... yes ... this could be diagnostic.

I pretended to be casual, looking at the menu. I thought through my list of friends from Claremont McKenna who were still in attendance, and picked someone I knew enough about that I could do some basic fact checking. "You wouldn't happen to know someone by the name of Ariel Sanchez, would you?"

Nancy immediately lit up. "Oh yeah. She's an absolutely awful person."

For a moment, I was very glad I hadn't said that she was a friend of mine. "Oh?" I looked back at her inquiringly.

Nancy continued, "Yeah, she cheated on her boyfriend."

I sat quietly. This was not the kind of information that I felt comfortable hearing secondhand about her. Nancy continued, "She's basically a terrible person."

I shuffled my silverware uncomfortably. "What makes you say that? The fact that she cheated?"

Nancy smiled a big grin once more, looking me right in the eye. I was starting to be a little frightened by that smile. "I dated the guy she cheated on, so I've heard a lot about her."

I nodded, staring at my empty plate. I wished our food had arrived so I could have something to distract me. "That ... makes sense."

Nancy continued, her voice rising slightly in intensity and her face becoming serious. "Plus everyone thinks she's a huge jerk. She went around her freshman year bragging about her SAT scores. Seriously, who does that?"

I looked up, frowning, and spoke quietly. "I mean, I know a lot of people who had some figuring out to do when they were a freshman. I am sure she's come a long way—"

Nancy cut me off. "She hasn't." Nancy wasn't smiling, and her tone left no room for negotiation.

I nodded once more. This conversation was not going well. However, I was willing to chalk things up to bad luck in choosing topics. A change of subject might get us out of the weeds. I tried my best to smile, being sure to make eye contact. "So what are you doing up here in the Bay?"

Nancy smiled back at me. "Working."

I spun my hand in small circles, gesturing for more information.

Nancy smiled and laughed. "So what do you do for fun?"

In case you haven't picked up on the pattern, the rest of the meal basically was her saying cryptic or unnerving things and then never explaining them, or just outright changing the topic anytime it landed on her. By the time our hour-long meal finished and we left the restaurant, I was fairly convinced that she was just messing with me, and I was exhausted from trying to keep up. I expected her to want to call it a night right there. Even if she didn't, I certainly did.

As we stepped out into the cold night air of San Francisco, she looked at me expectantly. "So, what do you want to do now?"

I looked back at her, slightly surprised. I now stood at a crossroads—I could throw in the towel or give it another go. I figured I only had time to lose. "Oh, um, well, I don't know, do you want to get a drink?"

She shook her head, and her grin faded only slightly as she made a frown. "No."

I thought hard. We needed to shake things up a bit. A new setting might fix that. An idea hit me. "How about we go to the beach in the sunset?"

Her eyes widened and her full smile returned. "You mean Ocean Beach? But it's like 9:30p.m!"

I nodded, smiling as well. "Yeah, let's do it!"

Nancy giggled, and her face brightened considerably. "Okay!"

Despite the two miles of distance between my car and us, she requested that we make the trek on foot. With that and the time it took to drive to the beach, which sat on the other side of the city, it was 10:30 p.m. when we arrived. By now the sun had completely set, but the waterfront remained surprisingly well populated, and about thirty other people milled around in our vicinity. As we stepped onto the glittering moonlit sands, the beach stretched as far as I could see in both directions. We discarded our footwear and took a seat on some concrete dividers.

As we looked down silently on the silica expanse before us, we noticed a few young people starting a campfire about halfway to the water. An icy breeze was freezing us both, and we huddled together to keep warm.

Nancy spoke first, staring fixedly at the flickering orange light on the sand. "That looks warm."

I turned to face her. "Yeah? Shall we go down and check it out?" It was more of a suggestion than a question.

Nancy shrugged. "I guess."

I raised an eyebrow, trying to parse her expression in the darkness. "Um, okay ... well, let's go then!"

We got up and trotted down the beach to where a small brazier burned fiercely against the whipping wind. A few young men crouched around it, trying to keep warm while sipping from aluminum beverage cans.

The portliest of them, a fellow with shaggy brown hair and a wild grin, greeted me heartily. "Hey, welcome! Grab a beer and sit around our fire! What are your names?"

A twenty-four-pack of PBR sat to my left and I grabbed one for myself, offering another to Nancy, who declined. "I'm Colin. This here is—"

Nancy cut me off abruptly. "Crystal."

I blinked, turning to face the person whose name I no longer knew. Crystal?

The shaggy one continued, "That's chill. I'm Dave. Where you guys from?"

Nancy—or should I say Crystal—continued, "We're visiting from Wisconsin. My brother works in the city setting up exhibits at the De Young Museum and I'm helping him out."

Dave smiled and maintained eye contact. "Right on—we're all art students here in San Francisco." He gestured broadly to the remaining campfire attendees. The other three guys around the fire nodded and held up their beers to greet us. But I was paying them no heed, for I was far too busy being thoroughly confused. Who in the heck was this girl I was sitting next to? What was this about being from Wisconsin? Why was I her *brother*? Was she trying to drop a hint?

We sat for about twenty minutes chatting with the art students. Nancy continued to spin a tale of our life in Wisconsin. I had no idea what to say to this, so I sat quietly and listened. Eventually Nancy grew tired of their company and motioned for us to head out, and I gladly obliged. As we walked up the beach, I wasted no time in investigating.

I looked at her harshly, my tone decidedly assertive. "Okay, so what the heck was going on there? What is your real name, anyway?"

Nancy smiled, giggling. "Nancy."

My tone grew more exasperated. "So why did you tell them your name was Crystal? Are you even from Wisconsin?"

Nancy shook her head. "Nope."

I furrowed my brow. "Could you please explain what is going on here?" I stopped walking and faced her, my mouth scrunched and my arms crossed.

Nancy's smile evaporated into a straight line and her eyes shed their warmth. She stopped walking as well. "I'm just having some fun, Colin. Don't be such a buzzkill—sheesh."

I stopped glaring and tried to decipher the meaning of her expression in the moonlight. She seemed genuinely put out. Not waiting for a response, she continued walking up the beach toward my car while I just stood there trying to make sense of it all. Maybe she was just a silly person who liked to mess with people a bit for fun. Was I being too uptight? Had I let my previous bad experiences change me for the worse?

I started into a quick jog and caught up to her, and as we climbed back into my car, she spoke up again. "So the last train left already. You're going to drop me off in Berkeley."

As I fumbled for my keys, I responded coolly. "Wow, that's really out of my way. I wish we'd kept better track of time. I didn't even think about what time the last train left."

Nancy smiled, leaning over and kissing me on the cheek. "Oh, it wasn't an accident. I knew I was going to miss it. I also knew you'd say yes to driving me home."

I froze with my seatbelt half on and shifted uncomfortably. I wasn't sure how to handle this—was she implying that I would be coming home with her tonight? And even if she was, did I want to join her? She had kind of been freaking me out.

Future Colin could make this decision in Berkeley. I responded absentmindedly, "Uh, yeah, okay."

Nancy giggled with glee and turned on the radio and began humming along to the music. It was merciful that we didn't have to talk on the way to her place, because I was spending the time trying to nail down my opinion of her.

As we got close to Berkeley, she flipped the radio off and gave me a very serious look.

"Just so we're clear, nothing is going to happen tonight. You're just dropping me off."

"Right." I nodded as I pulled off the freeway, feeling relieved but still irked that she had expected me to ferry her around the Bay without asking.

"Good." She turned the radio back on and resumed humming.

After dropping her off, I made the hour-long drive back to my house in Silicon Valley. Much to my surprise, I found that Marion and Vicky were still awake, despite it being 1:00 a.m. They were exceedingly curious about my date, so we all took a seat around our IKEA table and I relayed the evening's events, sparing none of the confusing and strange behavior I had witnessed.

As soon as I finished, Vicky took a hard stance. Her tone was serious, and her body language direct. She had seen me make enough bad dating decisions at this point to know I was prone to making some more. "This girl is clearly crazy. Don't see her again."

Marion didn't miss a beat on the combo, and her expression was one of concern as well. "Yeah, I mean she clearly stalked you before your date, plus she said a lot of rude and personal things about your friend Ariel. Not to mention the fact that she acted super sketchy."

Vicky took a more defensive posture now, turning to Marion. "Hey, I cyber-stalk people too. There's nothing wrong with that."

Marion's expression shifted to apologetic as she turned to Vicky and held up her palms. She then turned back to me and grew frowny again. "Regardless, all of the other things are huge red flags. Don't see her again. She gives me a super-bad vibe."

I nodded pensively as I listened to their opinions. What could I say—they were absolutely right. It sounded like a train wreck waiting to happen. I resolved not to text her for a second date and went to bed.

The next morning, I was immediately greeted with a text from Nancy:

"Would you be interested in playing some League of Legends with me?"

As I mentioned before, League of Legends was one of my favorite video games, and her interest in it was one of the things that had initially caught my attention. It's not important if you don't know what this game is—in fact it's probably for the best that we keep it that way on the off chance my description makes it sound AMAZING and your soul is sucked in by it, like mine. All you need to know is that it is a competitive multiplayer game, which many people liken to e-soccer.

Reading that text in the clarity of the morning, I immediately backtracked on my resolve from the night before. Doubt flooded my mind. What if I had just been too hard on her? What if she was totally normal and I had projected my own negative expectations upon her? I mean, let's be real for a moment—I can get carried away sometimes.

Once more, my rationale was simple: the only thing I had to lose was time.

Before I responded, I sent a text to Ariel, my friend from Claremont, whom I desperately needed to confirm that what Nancy had said about her was true. Hopefully she could vouch for the sanity of this girl, or at least warn me of possible trouble to come.

But Ariel's response was not timely. And without confirmation, I played League of Legends over the Internet with Nancy. It was a grand couple of hours. The strangeness of our previous encounter melted away beneath the magical teamwork that was our duo. We played exceptionally well together, and my prior concerns faded. Of course, this was not without its consequences—my roommates scowled at me from the hallway, crossing their arms and stomping as they went about their business, probably because they were a little sore that I was so blatantly disregarding our agreement of the night before. I waved away the doomsayers and continued my fun.

Naturally, this resounding success resulted in another date, although arranging it turned out to be something of a hassle. Eventually we decided that she would come over to my house on the coming Wednesday and we would play some more League of Legends. Why mess with a working formula, right?

By now, I had also heard back from Ariel, who verified that everything Nancy had said was indeed true. Ariel seemed to feel bad about how everything had gone down with her and Nancy's shared ex, and I felt sympathetic toward her. At the same time, I could see how these two people had come away from the situation with their respective viewpoints. For a moment, everything seemed to fit in a sane and logical manner.

When Wednesday came, Nancy caught the train down from the city, where she supposedly worked, and I picked her up at the last stop in Millbrae, a few miles from my house.

I greeted Nancy cheerfully, but after a bit of mild back-and-forth conversation, I had an issue I needed to resolve. "So Nancy, the last train leaves in just a couple of hours ... "

Nancy looked back at me, but I couldn't see her expression as I was driving. "I was planning on spending the night."

At this moment, we were taking a hard turn on a freeway on-ramp, and I nearly crashed the car in my surprise. Once I had recovered, I looked at her, shocked. "Whoa, all right then."

Nancy giggled. "I knew you would say yes."

I didn't know how to respond to this, so I said nothing. Of course, I was excited, but at the same time I still had reservations because of her previous behavior. After a minute, I realized there was a hitch. "Nancy, if things go well and you spend the night ... "

Nancy smiled. "They will."

I continued, "My product is being announced during our company's annual keynote tomorrow at 10:30 a.m. I NEED to be at work for that. It's very important. I'll happily get you an Uber back to the train station or something. But I can't be late. So, no sleeping in, okay?"

Nancy waved dismissively. "That's fine. I'm meeting up with someone in Redwood City tomorrow anyway. You said you live in downtown Redwood City, right?"

I nodded. "Yeah."

An awkward silence passed, and eventually I turned on the radio as we drove to my house. (By the way, if you ever have a second date that starts with an awkward silence, that's generally a Bad Sign. Capitalization for emphasis.)

We got to my house and set up our laptops at the kitchen table, quickly hopping into a game of League of Legends. I was somewhere between excited at the prospect of what might happen this evening and deeply concerned. Was she confident or crazy? I had no idea. While I was mulling this over, my roommates watched us grumpily from down the hallway, giving us inventive new versions of the stink eye for my continued flaunting of their disapproval. I responded in kind. Finally, Vicky had the boldness to come out and say hello. As she walked down the hallway, Nancy turned around at the sound of footfall. Vicky waved, and Nancy stood up.

Vicky extended a handshake. "Hi. I'm Vicky, one of Colin's housemates. I assume he mentioned us."

Nancy extended her hand as well. "Yeah, he did. I'm Jasmine. It's nice to meet you, Vicky."

Every muscle in my body – my heart, my lungs, my everything – came to a complete stop. From what I could tell, the same happened for Vicky: her nostrils flared, her eyes widened, and she looked in my direction with purpose. We made eye contact, neither of us breathing as we both watched the train that was my date go careening off the cliff.

Vicky turned back to Nancy, licking her lips as she took a deep breath. She spoke slowly and cautiously as she tried to collect herself. "Um ... I thought your name was Nancy?"

Nancy shook her head. She was still smiling politely and maintained her composure perfectly. "No, it's Jasmine."

I had gone to take a drink from a can of Mountain Dew, and I sputtered noisily, nearly dropping the can as I did so.

Vicky furrowed her brow, her tone serious and her volume low. "Look, Colin already told me your name was Nancy. He told us you were coming over tonight."

Nancy, or perhaps I should say Jasmine, continued smiling cordially as if they had just been discussing the weather. Her tone and face hinted at no concern whatsoever. "Ah, I see." Nancy turned around and returned to her seat at the table. "Shall we keep playing, Colin?"

Vicky and I stared at each other once more, both of us completely stunned. As I gathered what little cognitive function I still had, a furious look of purpose occupied Vicky's contorting face, one that came with more than a hint of indignation. She needed no words to describe what she was thinking: "GET HER OUT!"

I sat very quietly, very panicked. I didn't want to stand up and go have a private conversation with Vicky, because that would have been *rather uncomfortable* for Nancy. So, I shrugged and turned back to my computer. As I did, I was just able to catch a supernova of hate erupting from Vicky's eyes. I decidedly kept looking at my computer screen.

After a few seconds of furious silence, silence which must certainly have been the closest thing to a nuclear meltdown in California's history, Vicky stomped to her room at the end of the hallway. As I glanced after her, I caught an eyeful of Marion making frantic hand signs where Vicky had left off.

By this point, I didn't need the encouragement. If you had asked me if there was anything Nancy could say to salvage the situation, I would have said no. I would have said that the night was over and I was just trying to figure out how to end it.

I spoke softly. "Um, Nancy." My face was forged into a grimace.

Unlike mine, Nancy's voice was measured and rational, and she didn't even stop looking at her screen. "I'm just having a bit of fun with you and your roommate. I thought it was likely that you told them about the name thing at the beach. Can't you guys take a joke? Don't be such a buzzkill, sheesh."

I sat back in my chair, letting out a deep breath. If there was exactly one thing she could have said to explain herself out of that situation, that was it. Were my roommates and I overreacting? We did tend to do that.

As I ran my brain into overdrive trying to figure out what I should do about this, Nancy and I began playing League of Legends. The game went nothing shy of marvelously. Once more our teamwork was superb and our combo crushing. In fact, it went so well that I had completely forgotten about the whole name thing when we closed our laptops a couple of hours later. Enchanted by her gaming prowess, I headed back to my room with her.

Realizing that I would be facing more than a little heat from my roommates, I sent them a text explaining the situation. After brushing our teeth, Nancy and I headed over to my bed, where we started making out.

As my worries melted away, so did our clothes. Some foreplay led into me giving her head, and after a few minutes she told me that was enough. I reached under the bed and grabbed a condom.

Nancy looked at me very seriously for a moment. "What are you doing?"

I looked back at her, slightly confused. "Is this not what we're doing?"

Nancy looked downright shocked. "I never said we were having sex." She got up and started to put her clothes on. "Nope, it isn't happening."

I was disappointed, but I tried to keep my tone understanding, "Oh ... I see. I hope I didn't do something to make you uncomfortable."

Nancy shook her head. "No. I had no intention of having sex tonight."

I squinted my eyes and cocked my head slightly. "Um. Huh. You couldn't have told me that before we took our clothes off?"

Nancy crossed her arms, scoffing. "If you want to get off, why don't you just go in the bathroom and take care of yourself."

My concerned demeanor gave way to frustration as I crossed my arms. "Excuse me, but did you just tell me to go fuck myself?"

Nancy rolled her eyes. "If this is going to be a problem I can sleep on the couch."

I took a deep breath as I tried to figure out how to handle the situation. "Excuse me a moment."

I put my clothes on and stepped into the hallway. I was more than a little irked at her attitude, and I could feel my blood beginning to boil. Trying to cool down, I quietly talked it out with myself.

"She just likes fucking with people, right? Nothing to take personally. Be cool, Colin, there's no need to sweat it. You don't have to see her after tomorrow morning."

As I walked myself through it, I felt a lot better. I only had one concern at this point. I came back into the room.

"Nancy?"

Nancy was sitting on the bed, tapping at her phone. She turned to face me.

I met her eyes solidly, my expression serious. "If you do one thing for me, can you make sure you are out by nine-thirty tomorrow morning so I can be on time to my product announcement?"

Nancy rolled her eyes, her tone flippant. "*Duh*, I didn't forget."

I bit the rising desire to snap back, and responded as coolly as I could, "All right, I'll wake you up at 9:00 a.m. Is that enough time? I have an extra towel if you want to take a shower."

Nancy nodded, her voice sharp as she replied. "That's *fine*." I nodded my head and climbed into bed. Fortunately, it was spacious enough for two to sleep comfortably, and I was out within a minute.

The next morning, my alarm went off at 8:45 a.m. I took a lightning-quick shower and got dressed. At 9:00 a.m. exactly, I went to wake her up.

I placed my hand on her shoulder and shook her gently. "Nancy, its nine o'clock. You need to get up."

Nancy pulled away, mumbling at me, "Just get me up at nine-thirty when you need me to leave. I don't need a shower."

I wasn't in any mood to argue. I grabbed my laptop and walked out to the kitchen. At 9:25 I went back to Nancy and tried to wake her up again.

I placed my hand gently on her shoulder a second time. "It's time to go, Nancy."

Once more Nancy shook off my hand. "Fifteen more minutes."

My voice rose slightly in volume. "You're going to make me late."

Nancy sat up, scowling as her voice passed mine in irritation. "Look, I can just let myself out. Go to your meeting." She gestured forcefully at the door.

I frowned intensely. "There is no way I'm leaving you alone in my house."

Nancy threw herself back down onto the bed with a hard thump. "Well, that's YOUR choice," she muffled through a pillow.

At 9:45, 10:00, and 10:15 I tried to wake her up again. I figured if I was annoying enough she would get up and leave just to get me to stop bothering her. Each time she flatly told me to leave her alone. By now I knew there was no way I was making the product announcement. I texted my boss, letting him know that I would remotely watch the feed for the event from home. His response was less than pleased.

At 10:45 I contemplated next steps. I could call the police if I absolutely needed to, or I could wait this out as a war of attrition. Worst-case scenario, I could call Marion or Vicky to come deal with this. I thought through my options. Yep, this was worst-case scenario.

As I picked up my phone to text my roommates, Nancy stepped into the kitchen. I stood up as she entered the room, speaking quickly as I unplugged my work laptop. "Ready to go?"

Nancy ignored me and looked down at an empty bowl of oatmeal I had finished eating half an hour prior. Her voice and face were calm and composed, as if nothing was the matter. "I want some breakfast. Will you make me some oatmeal?"

I glared at her. "No. It's time to leave."

She rolled her eyes and walked over to my cabinets. "Fine, I'll make it myself."

I could hardly believe what I saw next. Systematically, she searched my cupboards for a bowl, a spoon, and an oatmeal packet. She prepared the mixture, placed it in the microwave, sat down, and started to eat. I was so shocked by her boldness I didn't even try to stop her.

She looked at my laptop, which still had the announcement for my product playing on it. The video feed showed the head of Oculus mobile giving a speech. She looked up at me, maintaining her calm and nonchalant demeanor. "Is that your launch thing?"

I didn't know what to say. I wasn't even bothered anymore. I was just stunned. I started grinning, and was on the brink of laughing hysterically, as I watched her eat oatmeal. She grew agitated and uncomfortable. "What are you doing? Why are you just watching me eat? This is really creepy."

I didn't say anything but continued staring at her bowl. My mind was racing. Had I brought this upon myself?

Nancy grew increasingly agitated. "All right, you are really freaking me out. I'm out of here." She stood up, collected her things, and left before I even realized what was happening.

As soon as I heard the closing door, I remembered that I was horrifyingly late to work. I closed my laptop, grabbed my bag, got into my car, and raced to the office. When I got to my desk, panting and out of breath, I immediately told my boss and coworkers what had happened, in far too much detail. I knew I was in hot water for missing such an important event, so I figured telling the truth might do some real damage control. And although my manager looked rather disappointed when I first walked in the door, they were all absolutely delighted to hear my story. They had heard about some of my previous dating misadventures, and at this one they were positively salivating. A million and one questions flew at me: What's her real name? Can we see a picture? Have you told your roommates about this morning yet? Most important, the question formed around when—not if—date three would happen. I now had a question of my own: Why did they have such little faith in my decision-making ability?

When I got home from work, my housemates were unshockingly mad that I had let Nancy spend the night. Both were waiting for me in the living room when I stepped through the front door.

Marion kicked things off. "I CAN'T BELIEVE YOU LET A CRAZY PERSON STAY OVERNIGHT IN OUR HOUSE! What were you thinking?!" She flailed her arms angrily, and a deep frown sat in her burgundy-colored face.

Vicky followed up. "Oh, wait, you *weren't* thinking. Or should I say you were thinking with your dick?"

I looked hard at Vicky and Marion. "Guys, come on. There was no way to know that she wasn't going to leave this morning."

Marion sighed dramatically, throwing up her arms as she stormed out of the living room. "He's hopeless."

Vicky waved a finger at me. "You know what: I don't even care. She's banned from our house."

I nodded. "Yeah, all right. That sounds fair."

From her bedroom, Marion shouted back at us, "And make him promise not to see her again! She's clearly crazy!"

Vicky's eyebrows rose. "Oh yeah, that too."

I rolled my eyes. "Yeah, yeah, I know. You don't need to convince me. I promise I won't see her again."

Vicky shook her head forcefully. "Nuh-uh. Pinky promise." She held out a finger.

I let out an exasperated sigh. "Oh come on."

Vicky glared at me, jabbing me in the side forcefully with her little finger.

"Hey! Okay, fine." I joined my finger with hers. "I pinky-swear I won't see her again."

Vicky nodded cordially. "Good."

Of course, this agreement was entirely perfunctory; I had already firmly decided that I would not see Nancy again. After all that had happened, what sane man would? (Ladies and gentlemen, if you hadn't figured it out by now, I am not a sane man.)

Later that day, Nancy called. I shouldn't have answered, but I did.

Her tone was calm and sincere. "Hey, Colin. I'm sorry for how I acted last night and this morning. That was totally inappropriate of me. I feel awful. Even if you don't want to see me again, I liked playing League of Legends with you and I would like to at least do that. No more name shenanigans. I'll be normal."

I didn't say anything.

Her voice trembled. It was almost apprehensive. "Can you please just give me another shot? Just one?" I could hear genuine sorrow. Something about her tone sounded eerily familiar, but I couldn't place it.

"You there, Colin?"

I realized that I was hearing the voice of a lonely Carlsbad game designer. One who had screwed up and wanted to make things right with his ex.

I let out a long sigh. "Yeah, I'm here. I'll let you know."

By now, I had sort of figured out that she was an expert at manipulating people. I mean, literally everything she did pointed to that. But in a lot of ways, I saw myself in the way she apologized. I remembered how sorry I felt when I had called Stella those months ago, how much it hurt when she turned me down. I just didn't have the heart to do that to Nancy, especially after what sounded like genuine remorse. I figured we could at least play League of Legends over the Internet together. That had gone well.

So, that's what we did. I reached out to her for a game of League of Legends, and we played. It was a blast, like always. Later that week she followed up for a couple more games. We played and we had fun. She was a superb gaming buddy.

At the end of this last session she made a tentative proposal. "So, how would you feel about coming up to my house this Friday night to play League of Legends in person?"

We were on Skype audio, and I said nothing.

Nancy seemed downright sweet, almost sad, as she spoke. "I really like playing with you, Colin. Just come over and give it another shot. Please? No shenanigans, I promise."

I sat quietly, thinking. If I drove, I could leave at any time. I would park around the block so she didn't know where my car was. Assuming she didn't assault me, what did I have to lose? Time? If we kept it to League of Legends, it seemed like the night should go well.

"All right," I conceded.

Nancy giggled in delight, and I imagined that she was smiling as broadly as ever.

Of course, my motivation to go over was more than just to play League of Legends. In the back of my mind, I secretly hoped that maybe the first two dates had just been a rough start. The pickings had been mercilessly slim in Silicon Valley, and even if the odds of things working out were microscopic, those were odds I was willing to take.

Unfortunately, I had a lot of work to do that Friday, so I couldn't leave Facebook HQ until 9:00 p.m. I messaged her when I left the office, letting her know that it would take an hour to reach her place in San Francisco. After parking and everything, I walked up to the tall oaken doors of her row house at 10:00 p.m. on the nose. (By the way, I have no idea why she had me drop her off in Berkeley after our first date if she lived in San Francisco. It didn't occur to me until I wrote this of the mismatch.)

Nancy answered the door immediately. After we exchanged hellos, she led me up the creaking set of stairs just beyond the door. At the top, a long hallway led us to the kitchen. Once there she gestured for me to take a seat at a small table barely big enough for two. As I settled in and looked around, I noticed her house was much like the other hundred-plus-year-old row houses that populated San Francisco. It was tall and narrow, with plaster walls and Victorian stylings, a combination that lent it an antique feel.

As my eyes found their way over the kitchen counter, I noticed a man in his late twenties playing the video game Destiny on an Xbox One in the living room. He paid me no heed; either he didn't notice me or didn't care to introduce himself. I presumed him to be one of her roommates.

As I took in my surroundings, I could hear the clicking of a burner, and I turned to see Nancy placing a skillet on the stove. I raised my eyebrows in surprise, my tone somewhat apologetic. "Oh—I didn't know you were cooking dinner for us. I already ate like ... hours ago. I'm sorry, I wouldn't have eaten if I had known."

Nancy didn't turn around, but instead started filling a large pot in the sink. "This is for me, not you." She placed the pot on a second burner, turning it to high.

I thought for a moment, parsing what she said. "Oh, did you just get home?"

Nancy shook her head, still facing the counter. She pulled out a knife and began chopping a bell pepper. "Nope." She nonchalantly poured some olive oil into the skillet and placed the freshly chopped pepper into it.

As I watched the steam rise from the pot, I seriously contemplated my decision to see her for a third time. While there was nothing wrong with her making dinner for herself, it seemed very odd for her to decide to do it once I came over, especially if she wasn't planning on including me. I couldn't put my finger on exactly why, but something about the situation just didn't feel right.

Nancy gave the skillet a few shakes, then came over and sat down. She immediately noticed my downcast demeanor. "So. Do you like whiskey?"

My frown evaporated and my eyebrows shot up. "Uh, yeah, actually. Quite a bit."

Nancy stood and walked over to the cabinet, pulling out a bottle of top-shelf whiskey. I don't remember the exact brand, but I recognized it to be one that I had had before. She pulled out two tumblers and poured us each a couple of fingers. Wordlessly, she placed one on the table in front of me and took the other back over to the stove. She placed pasta in the water and stirred the vegetables.

As I sipped from my tumbler, my face bore an expression of pleasant surprise. "Wow ... you have really nice taste in whiskey. I must say, I'm impressed. This is quite the treat."

Nancy cast a glance over her shoulder. "Yeah, don't drink too much of it."

I chuckled. "Worried I'm going to drink you out of house and home?"

Nancy continued stirring her meal, casting a glance to the now-empty couch in the living room where the man had been. "No, it's my roommate's. If you only have a little, he won't notice."

I nearly spit out my whiskey in surprise. "Seriously?"

Nancy turned from the pot to face me. Her face was now one of concern. "Look, I'm sorry about making you watch me make dinner, and honestly, my roommate doesn't care that much if you have some of his whiskey. Let me finish cooking and we can play a game of League of Legends. You'll feel better."

I sighed. "Yeah, okay."

Nancy turned back to the stove. Within a minute or two, her food was done and she was eating it at the table. I silently watched her eat. It was an awkward ten minutes.

Finally, she finished and beckoned me to follow her down the hallway. As she turned the knob on what I assumed was her room, I stopped in the hallway, considering for a moment that this seemed like a Very Bad Idea. "We're going to your room?"

Nancy turned around, rolling her eyes. "My table is not big enough for two laptops." She continued through the door and beckoned me to follow.

Her room matched the proportions of the rest of the house, being barely large enough for a full-sized mattress and a cramped desk, and the only available space for sitting was on said mattress. We both took a seat with our back to the wall and unpacked our computers. Sure enough, once we started playing League things got better. I had a lot of fun.

After the first game finished we had a break while we waited for the second one to queue up. We were both in good spirits from having crushed our opponents, and as I untangled my mouse cord, she moved in for a kiss. Feeling optimistic, I reciprocated. She moved our laptops and wrapped her legs around me, going in for several more smooches the whole time. As I starting engaging more, she abruptly stopped.

She pulled her head back and looked at me, neither smiling nor frowning, stating in a very matter-of-fact manner, "You know, Colin, I think I like you just as a friend."

At that I had finally had enough. "Get off me." My voice was unmistakably determined. I pulled at her legs as I tried to free myself, but she tightened her grip. "Let go of me, Nancy!"

Nancy started pleading, "Oh come on, don't be like that."

I raised my voice. "I SAID LET GO OF ME."

Nancy glanced nervously at the door and loosened her grip. I pulled myself free and hurriedly grabbed my laptop and jacket. I was at the door before Nancy could even get up.

"Colin, wait. I'm ... I'm sorry," she pleaded.

I turned around, tears in my eyes, my voice shaking as I sarcastically quipped, "Yeah, me too."

With that, I went down the stairs and out the front door. I never turned around, and I never looked back.

Naturally, my roommates and coworkers were very curious about the outcome of this third date, but I felt so embarrassed and ashamed that I refused to tell anyone what had happened. The whole experience left me feeling worthless and used, and frankly I didn't have a lot of self-respect for a while after that.

Looking back, I should have trusted my friends on this one. However, the dating world of Silicon Valley had warped my mindset. Since cute, intelligent software girls were in short supply, the fear of missing out on someone like Nancy was much higher than the fear of wasting my time with someone whom I didn't think it would work out with. This experience ultimately made me realize that my time was cheap relative to a woman's, and that I had to be careful not to get burned by this power dynamic when dating in such a stilted environment.

Jaipur

"T HE DEFENSE HAS BROKEN into the pocket! The quarterback throws the ball ... " A manly voice crackles over an antique radio as you sit in eager anticipation. "The ball is in the air ... it's a Hail Mary!"

The announcer's raspy words intensify as the broadcast continues. You are now on your feet, clutching the radio with both hands. "The receiver has made the catch! He's crossing the thirty! The twenty! The ten! TOUCHDOWN!" The distant sounds of cheering and stomping can be heard as you jump up and down exuberantly.

Except this isn't a football game. This a completely different kind of Hail Mary. Remember how in the first paragraph of this book I asked you to hold a thought? No? I'll wait for a moment while you go back and look that up. Back? Yep, we're finally doing it! It's time for a story about a game of Jaipur.

Let's start with our main character, Caroline. Caroline is a razor-thin, average-height software engineer from my hometown of Seattle, who moved to Silicon Valley around January of 2015, just a few months before me, for a new job at a stealth-mode tech startup.

I am hard pressed to come up with a more perfect characterization of the word "mousy" than her. She is quiet and shy, tending to not make her presence known in conversation unless around people she's intimately familiar with. Her black hair is ruler-straight, and her nervous posture and slight figure give the impression of great fragility.

Still, I feel this description doesn't quite do her justice, so if you want to get a good picture of her you are going to need to think of the mousiest elements of all the mousy people you know and kind of amalgamate them into one corporeal being. I don't recommend conjuring up images of mousy guys for this mental exercise, as the next part of this story is just going to get weird. Unless of course you are into that kind of thing, in which case, knock yourself out.

I don't recall exactly how well Caroline and I knew each other when we both lived in Seattle, but given that we had several mutual friends from Microsoft, I think it's safe to say that we knew each other existed and had bumped into each other at parties. One of these mutual friends, Armen, had moved to Silicon Valley just ahead of us. Around the start of the summer of 2015, he formally introduced me to Caroline, which marked the start of our friendship. An avid gamer like myself, Caroline and I quickly bonded over bouts of King of Tokyo and The Binding of Isaac (the second one was more just me watching her play).

Over that summer and the coming fall, our friendship grew, and I developed an interest in Caroline. She was articulate, generous, and had an amazing way of communicating nonverbally. It was as if she had developed an entire language made up entirely of facial expressions and hand gestures. Gaining an understanding of this language took time, but as a wild gesticulator myself, I eventually caught on.

Plus, I was still raw from those brutal few weeks with Nancy, and Caroline's warmheartedness became a form of Neosporin. Unlike Nancy, she went out of her way to make people feel special. She would call me up, asking if I wanted to bake a cake with her, and when I showed up, we would actually bake a cake. Or sometimes, she would just bake something and share it with me while we played board games.

Conceivably enough, I had gotten a vibe that she was also interested in me, and after a while I decided to try my luck one night and see if I could strike a spark. With a phrase like "try my luck" you might be mistakenly imagining a romantic evening filled with roast duck, fine wines, dramatic hair flips, and sly winks over a candlelit table, all under the stars and to the smooth sounds of a live saxophonist. And when I say "live saxophonist" I don't mean just any saxophonist; this is Kenny G himself.

Well, if this is what you are imagining, then it's not quite right. Instead, imagine us seated on a worn-out couch in Caroline's smallish three-bedroom apartment, and me sheepishly turning to her and asking, "So, are you like … into me or what?" Quite suave if I say so myself. Sadly, her equally awkward response was, "Ehhhhh … I thought I might be, but now I don't think so."

Ouch.

Bruised ego aside, I wasn't about to throw away our friendship over the rejection, and the two of us continued to hang out as if nothing had happened. And from my point of view, all of this was

A-OK. Even if things never progressed romantically, I was enjoying having a girl in my life who wasn't messing with my head.

However, things took an inevitable turn when we were both invited to one of Armen's friend's houses for a nineties-themed party in mid-December of 2015. By this point, I had fully accepted that Caroline and I were just friends, and I had shifted my attention to another girl who would be in attendance: Amy. By a stroke of coincidence, Amy navigated the same circles as Armen, and the two of us had something of a brief history from high school, which I was hoping to rekindle. I sent her a text the day before to test the water:

Me: "Hey, I heard there's a costume party this weekend. Can I look forward to seeing you there?"

Her: "Haha, you most certainly can. ;)"

Sweet baby Jesus, she sent a winky face. A promising sign, to be sure.

Given that the party was a solid hour away, Caroline, Armen, and a few of his friends all decided to meet at my house, cram into my gray 2011 Ford Focus, and shuttle on over to the hootenanny. If we are being entirely honest, I am not exactly sure what a hootenanny is, but if a bunch of drunk people in silly costumes carousing doesn't qualify, then I think the word needs to be redefined to fit those parameters.

Regardless of what you'd like me to call it, when we arrived at the party, Caroline immediately stuck herself to me. And I'm not talking a little bit stuck, like slightly tacky syrup on your fingers. I mean like the handle of a sink to your hand when you use too much superglue and get distracted while fixing everything in your apartment before a landlord inspection (which did actually happen to me once). To put it more concretely, Caroline was always by my side, touching my arm, asking if I wanted to go over and try the punch or talk to so-and-so, and generally acting like a girlfriend would. In fact, it was so overt that pretty much everyone at the party was shooting me looks like "Oh, are you two together?" No one directly asked, thank goodness, because I probably would have done something boneheaded like turn to her and ask, "Yeah, what exactly is going on here, anyway?"

Despite this perplexing situation, Caroline had previously made it clear she wasn't interested, so when we eventually ended up apart I made a point to seek out Amy. Given that this was a themed party, I was dressed to impress (as Kurt Cobain, no less) and turned on the charm machine. (I like to imagine a charm machine as an intricate puzzle box with the ghost of Prince inside, which whispers me smooth pickup lines. But I digress.)

As I walked up to Amy, I did my best to appear casual. I smiled just a hint as I spoke, hoping to appear intrigued but not too eager. In the back of my head, Prince's silky-smooth voice reminded me to be cool.

I took a deep breath, making sure to make eye contact. "Hey Amy, how's it going?"

Amy looked up from the platter of layered bean dip she had been examining, a pita chip in one hand and a completely neutral expression on her face. "Oh, fine," she replied coolly. "Shouldn't you be asking Caroline that, though?" Her eyes narrowed as she spoke, her tone pointed.

I nervously rubbed the back of my neck, forcing an awkward smile. "I'm not sure I follow."

"Oh, well, it seems like you two are having a great time *together.*" Amy raised her eyebrows to match the emphasis on the last word.

I sharply drew my next breath. "I know this is going to sound like a total cop-out, but the way she is acting is as surprising to me as it is to you. I don't know what the heck is going on." I made a shrugging gesture and bit my lip.

Amy turned to leave, smirking sardonically as she placed a hand on my shoulder. "Well, I hope you enjoy your surprise."

Okay, so "coolly" may have been sugarcoating things a bit; that was liquid nitrogen (believe me, I know). And to be perfectly honest, I am not completely sure why she was so frosty with me, though it would certainly appear it was because she accurately read my text message as testing for interest. Defeated, I milled around the party while trying to have a good time. In fact, I would say that I had a blast, all things considered. But, given that I had to drive my crew home that evening, I wasn't drinking too much. And I wasn't the only one metering my drinks. Oddly enough, Caroline was also taking the alcohol on the slow, which really meant that she was not drinking *anything* alcoholic. I didn't think too much of it, other than it denied me of an obvious explanation for her girlprending (portmanteau of girlfriend and pretend—snazzy, no?).

Eventually, the night grew late and the festivities wound down. My crew and I piled back into my Ford Focus and I returned us to Redwood City. As we drove home, I tried to make sense of the evening. Caroline had made it clear that she wasn't interested before, so why was she acting like this now? Had she changed her mind? I dismissed the thought immediately; it was best not to get my hopes up about these kinds of things.

We got back to my place around 1:30 a.m., at which point everyone was sleepy, exhausted, and ready to go home. That is, everyone except Caroline. Whereas the others edged in the direction of their cars, she hung back with me. Everyone else, not wanting to be rude, waited up for her as she dawdled.

Armen finally spoke up. "Caroline, are you coming?"

Caroline looked at the ground, then at me, as she mumbled, "Ummm ... yeah. I just ... uh ... "

I knew a cue when I saw one, and I deftly jumped in. "Oh, do you want to hang out for a bit to sober up?"

Caroline nodded vigorously, and the others walked off totally uncurious about what was not-so-subtly going on. (Thank goodness I hang out with socially oblivious engineers who don't pick up on that kind of thing!)

At this point, it probably goes without saying that I was stoked. Clearly, during our many days spent together I had won her over with my dazzling charm and good looks, and to boot she'd come to this conclusion without the influence of alcohol (to be clear, I am not implying that in other situations I get girls drunk to sleep with me). But as she sheepishly followed me into the house, I noticed that that very same sobriety was leaving her more than a little nervous.

Once we were inside my warm living room, I casually leaned against my wall, looking at Caroline using the most seductive face I could muster. "Hey, Caroline, can I get you something to drink? A cocktail or some wine? We could throw on a TV show or something and I can grab a blanket."

Caroline shot me a confused expression, standing at a fair distance and showing no intention of closing it. "Um, no, that's okay."

I stood up straight, a little confused. My suave expression melted into one of perplexity. "Huh, all right. So, what exactly were you planning on coming in for then? I know you didn't have anything to drink."

Caroline walked over to my bookshelf, which was stuffed silly with board games. "Can we play one of these?"

Caught off guard, I dropped my hands to my side. "What?"

Caroline ignored the question, opting to instead continue exploring my collection. Worse yet, she was looking at the long games—the ones of the forty-five- to ninety-minute variety.

I shook my head in disbelief. "Whoa, whoa, whoa. This isn't happening. It's nearly two in the morning. We're not playing a board game." By now I was confused, thoroughly tired, and way too sober for these kinds of shenanigans.

Caroline stopped browsing and crossed her arms while she pouted at me fitfully.

I let out a long sigh. "Fine, but I'm picking a short one."

I reached down and picked up the quickest two-player game I owned, Jaipur. For those who haven't played, it's a fast-paced token-and-card game where each round takes about five minutes. It's a lot of fun, especially if you are looking for something short and strategic in the sparsely populated two-player category. My one piece of advice, if you do play, is that you must make sure you finish with the prestigious "Panda Camel," which is something that will make a lot more sense once you have played the game. (Note to editor: if this book becomes super popular and Jaipur sells a bunch, remind me to hit up the people who made it for a beer. And if you guys are reading, I mean an expensive one too—don't go cheap on me!)

Fortunately, as I held up Jaipur, Caroline responded with a smile and a nod of the head. Sighing in relief, I put the game under my arm and motioned down the hallway. "Shall we go to my bedroom to play?"

To be clear, this was not a come-on. The living room in my Redwood City house was a serious echo chamber, and you could clearly hear even the softest whispers in each of the bedrooms. I was doing this more out of consideration to my roommates than anything.

Caroline shot me a suspicious look and crossed her arms. "What exactly are you trying to pull here, bub?"

I rubbed my eyes, letting out a drawn-out groan. "Look, Caroline, I'm tired. I just want to go to bed. But if you have your heart set on a game we can do that. However, I'm not going to stack on waking up and annoying my roommates. And that's exactly what will happen if we play out here. Either we go to my room or we don't play. Your call."

Caroline mulled over the idea, and eventually she shrugged her shoulders and began walking toward my room.

This is where things are about to get interesting. Let's set the stage. Caroline and I are sitting on my bed at about 1:45 a.m. playing Jaipur on a Saturday night. I am tired, confused, slightly disappointed, and still slightly aroused from the apparent miscommunication earlier. What I had thought was an evening of intrigue leading up to our inevitable slip into romance was turning into an exhausting marathon of platonic patience. I can only imagine that she was feeling most of those emotions, except probably also on guard because we were sitting on my bed.

Yet, after playing Jaipur for some five minutes, she put her cards down and looked at me with a blank expression. "Do you want to just like ... try kissing?"

I put my hand down as well, trying to contain a bizarre mix of excitement and confusion that was taking over my face. "What? I mean, yeah. But, didn't you ... I mean, yeah, let's do it!" I failed to contain my smile, which grew even larger, seemingly with a will of its own.

We both leaned in for a kiss. You could feel the love in the air—sparks were positively flying (cue the Kenny G!). Yet right as our lips touched something felt very, VERY, wrong. Instead of kissing me, she ... well ... I don't know to describe it other than saying that she robot-faced me! Crazy, right? What? You don't know what that is?

Okay, to explain this, I want you to imagine that you are about to kiss a mannequin. When you kiss it, what does it do? It does nothing! It's an inanimate object. That's what inanimate objects do. And that's basically what she did. If you aren't sure why this is so alarming to have happen, and you have someone you can kiss, have them keep a completely straight face and not react at all as you both lean in. I promise that it will be an unsettling experience.

As soon as I felt this total lack of response, I sharply pulled back, my expression one of alarm. "What just happened?" Having never been robot-faced before, I was thoroughly confused and unsettled, unsure what to make of the experience.

Caroline tightened her lips as I looked down to the side. She shrugged amicably. "I'm sorry... I just wasn't feeling it. Can we keep playing our game?"

I stared blankly back at her as she picked up her hand. At this point I was feeling all the same confused, aroused, and disappointed emotions as before, except now significantly more of them. But, without a clear alternative option, I picked up my hand and we kept playing.

After another two minutes of ridiculously uncomfortably silence, she put down her hand again. She looked up at me with a completely straight face and said, "Do you want to just take our clothes off and see what happens?"

Now, my jaw was hanging slackly. I quickly scooped it up and tried to play it off like Mr. Cool. "Uh. Yeah. I'd be okay with that."

Caroline smirked, clearly seeing through my weak attempts at remaining chill. "Yeah? You'd be okay with that? *Just* okay with that? If I had to guess, I would say you look like you are a little more excited than 'just okay with that.'"

What could I say? She was dead on the money. To be fair, I was probably grinning like an idiot, so it wasn't like she was a savant. All things considered, I think my giddiness was well justified, as this was a pretty big windfall and seemed to be a sure sign of good things to come.

Without any further ado, we both stood up and took off all our clothes.

Now, you might be trying to imagine exactly how this went down. To say the least, it was an awkward affair. Have you ever tried stripping naked in front of someone you have never been naked with before, or done anything with other than share an exceptionally awkward kiss moments prior? It's a weird experience. On par with the robot face, except less alarming and more uncomfortable. I don't recommend trying it.

Awkwardness aside, I was still definitely (and visibly) stoked as we sat back down on the bed. At this point I was thinking, "Aw yeah, this is gonna be great," and I was mentally gearing up for foreplay. Let's emphasize the word "was," because it very quickly stopped being true when she picked up her cards again.

I blinked at Caroline, tilting my head as I looked from her cards to her face, and then back to her cards. I studied her expression, trying to figure out what was going through her head. Meanwhile, she continued looking at her hand, her face totally neutral. After a few seconds, she played a card. I looked at both of us, confirming that yes, we were in fact naked.

I tried to think of something to say. At a complete loss, I figured I should just keep playing and let her take things at her pace. So, I picked up my cards and resumed playing. Another two long long minutes passed before she put her hand down for a third time.

As she did, she looked me dead in the eye. For the life of me I have no idea what her face was telling me, but it involved a smile, a frown, and scrunchy eyebrows. If I had to guess, I would say it was expressing some mixture of discomfort and sexual interest. "Do you want to try kissing again?" she asked softly.

Shaking my head in disbelief, I put my hand down as well. "Uh. Yeah, okay."

We both leaned in.

The instant our lips touched, I recoiled back in alarm. "YOU ROBOT-FACED ME AGAIN? WHY DO YOU KEEP DOING THIS?!"

She now looked off to the side, scrunching up her whole face. Her cheeks grew flush, as if she was about to cry. "Can we try to do it ... without kissing? Would that be okay?"

I immediately regretted reacting so sharply. Perhaps she was simply inexperienced, although I knew that she had dated before. I had no idea what the right play was, and I figured it would be best to err on the side of caution.

"Yeah, okay, sure." I rubbed the back of my neck nervously. "Do you want to lie down?"

She nodded and lay down on her back. Fortunately, extensive reading had convinced me of the importance of foreplay, and successful field trials had made me rather confident in my abilities regarding this stage of the lovemaking process. In fact, I would say that I was quite competent at administering female pleasures. However, every time I tried to kiss her neck, or nibble her ear, or do anything romantic at all, she either didn't react or pulled away sharply.

Sitting up, tired and defeated, I asked her for clarification. "Is something wrong, Caroline?"

She sat up as well and looked off in the distance with a slight frown. Without a word, she lay back down, curled up in the fetal position, and started crying.

Whoa. This took a turn I did not expect. And now I was feeling like a real jerk.

I reached over to place a hand on her shoulder, which she shook off. "Do you want to talk, Caroline?"

She didn't say anything.

I waited for a few seconds, my voice as soft and compassionate as I could make it. "Would you like a hug?"

No response.

I cleared my throat. "How about a glass of water?"

Nope. Nada.

As I sat there contemplating what the heck I should do, I could hear her softly crying. After a few minutes, she went silent, and after another few minutes, with me still sitting there like a dope scratching my head, I noticed that her breathing had changed. I leaned over, and sure enough, she was asleep.

So here I was, sitting naked on my bed with a half-finished game of Jaipur strewn about the sheets. On the other side of the bed, Caroline was also naked, and asleep. Completely at a loss as to what I should do next, I did the only sane thing I could think of: I called my mom.

I'm just kidding! Good god, could you imagine how my mom would have reacted if I had called her at 2:00 a.m., described the situation, and asked her for advice? I think it's safe to say that that phone call would have gone rather poorly. Instead, I cleaned up the board game, put on some boxers and a T-shirt, crawled into bed, and went to sleep as well.

At around eight the next morning, Caroline woke up. It was one of those "Oh my god, where am I, why am I naked, and what on earth is going on?" wake-ups. This surprised me, given that she had been stone-cold sober the night before and only had herself to blame for the situation she now found herself in.

She quickly stood up and began gathering her clothes. As she was getting dressed, I sat up and asked groggily, "What *happened* last night?"

She didn't say anything, but continued hurriedly dressing herself.

Realizing that our time together was on a short clock, I stood up and walked over to her. "Seriously, you can't just leave me hanging here."

Now fully clothed, she turned to face me, wearing a sad frown and weary eyes. "I thought I would be interested in you, but I guess I just wasn't." And with that, and me standing there at a loss for anything to say, she left my house.

To this day that was the only explanation I ever received. I tried to get her to talk about it, but she seemed pretty set on not doing so.

Now, in a normal city with normal gender ratios you might imagine that an *extremely* awkward encounter like that would result in us avoiding each other. At the very least, you must imagine it would put a gigantic strain on our friendship.

Unfortunately, Silicon Valley is not normal. When you're a male software engineer in Silicon Valley, you quickly find that your female friends are worth their weight in gold. Even if you have no interest in them, just having some female contact is important to staying sane. Plus, they generally attract other women to hang out with you. In fact, the gender ratios are so skewed that many women in tech also have a problem finding women to socialize with, so having at least one woman in a friend group can be a huge boon to getting more, one of whom you might click with.

Given what I just said, it probably comes as no surprise that I made it a point to make sure Caroline still felt welcome after everything that happened. In fact, our friend group with Armen continued unhindered, minus the fact that Caroline and I didn't hang out one-on-one anymore. The only real lasting consequence has been that anyone who has heard this story will NOT use my Jaipur set. (To me this makes no sense. It's not like we were having sex on it or using it during sex. I mean, we didn't even have sex! Plus, I'm not even sure how you would incorporate something like that into lovemaking ... like maybe use the tokens?)

Anything Once

I T WAS A COLD DARK NIGHT on the streets of Seattle. Scratch that. Before we start this one, let's rewind to the start of the summer of 2015. In case you are struggling with the time line, this was about two and a half months after I had moved to Silicon Valley.

You may recall that as the summer started, I was freshly heart-broken at losing the love of my life, Stella. You may also recall that I was navigating the choppy waters of my new clandestine affair with Mindy. I was certainly in a place to make some more bad decisions. Fortunately for that, the interns had just arrived at Facebook's campus. For those who are unfamiliar with the software industry, the summers are absolutely packed with interns. But it's not the car-washing kind of slave job that *Silicon Valley* the TV show makes it out to be. In tech, interns are generally expected to make meaning-ful contributions, and on software engineering teams they usually get the choice coding projects. I haven't ever worked outside of the software industry, so I can't say how it is for the rest of the world, but

I would guess this is a somewhat unique phenomenon, which stems from the fact that there is a huge demand for software professionals and a relatively scarce labor market. This forces tech companies to respond in much the same way the global tobacco industry markets to its clients: get 'em young and make 'em count.

Before we continue, I need to clear something up. You're probably thinking that, with all this talk of bad decision-making, I am about to tell a tale of preying on some interns. Just what kind of guy do you think I am? After all we have been through, do you think I am capable of something like that? I am appalled at your insinuation. Appalled, I say. Okay, maybe I should get along with the story before you decide to put this book down and start writing me death threats for being such a god-awful creeper.

This would probably also be a good time to mention that Armen—the mutual friend Caroline and I shared—works for Facebook. From time to time, the two of us would get lunch together at work, although not too frequently because he sat basically on the other end of campus from me. Usually this involved me tagging along with his team on their typical lunch journey.

In early June, his team's new intern started showing up, a girl by the name of Chelsea. (Should I say "woman"? I'm never sure how to classify females in their early twenties. I am sure someone will send me a strongly worded email if I screw this up. Thanks in advance.) By this point you probably could have guessed that a female software engineering intern is something of a rare thing. But in case I haven't beaten you over the head with the stilted-gender-ratio point enough already, trust me when I say that you would be very hard pressed to find a software company where less than 80% of the engineers are men. So, when Chelsea, a short female engineering intern with long brown hair, a slightly athletic vibe, and a warm, bubbly demeanor became a part of the lunch group, you can probably (and correctly) guess that she got a lot of attention.

I know this paints Facebook and the software industry in a pretty bad light, where a bunch of older dudes are hitting on a few younger girls. However, I just want to say that compared to every other tech company I have seen or worked at, Facebook and Oculus have the most dignified treatment of women. That does not say much, though. The implication here is that engineers hitting on women, or at the very least giving them undue attention, is an industry-wide phenomenon (*cough* problem), which is best illustrated with an example.

When I started as a full-timer in Seattle at Microsoft Game Studios in 2013, I was part of a large group of college hires who rotated between existing teams within the division, such as 343 Industries (which makes Halo), Turn 10 Studios (which makes Forza Motorsport), and Microsoft Publishing (which makes everything else). This post-collegiate rotation program no longer exists, but at the time it was well populated with engineers, designers, and artists, fresh-faced and excited to have broken into a notoriously difficult-to-enter video game industry.

On the team where I was placed for my first rotation, there was one rather attractive female, Irene, who garnered some attention from both the new and old hires. She was tall and slender and had silky smooth brown hair that flowed just below her shoulder line. Her face was angular but feminine, and her eyes and personality glowed with more fire than almost anyone else's I have ever met. Without a doubt, she was a head-turner, and at a normal company I would hope that this would have been worthy of little more than a passing remark. Unfortunately, at this organization it became more of an obsession.

Almost without exception, when she would walk by the engineering area—where many of the rotating college-hire engineers sat—a conversation would start up. The conversation below is fictitious, but representative of how these would typically go:

As Irene walked by, Kenneth, the engineer closest to the hallway, craned his neck to make sure the coast was clear. He turned back to the group, grinning hungrily. "Man, she is so hot."

Cameron snickered, casting a wry smile back at Kenneth. "I know, right? Do you think I have a chance with her?"

"You wish." Kenneth failed to contain a laugh, turning to another engineer. "You think he can pull it off, Arnold?"

Arnold shook his head. "No way. She doesn't even know you exist."

Kenneth held up his hands, making a curvy-woman shape with them as he spoke. "What I would do to that ... "

Arnold rolled his eyes, turning back to his keyboard. "Keep dreaming. I think I might ask her out at some point." The other two guys laughed.

As crazy as this sounds, this kind of discussion was typical in response to something as mundane as Irene simply walking by a group of younger men. I got ridiculously used to hearing conversations like this. Sometimes they would be tame like that, and other times they would be much less safe for work. And this was not limited to my immediate peers. People on other floors and in other parts of the games division would talk about Irene as if she was the ultimate quest. It was as if there was a semi-public contest that only happened when she, another woman, or a manager wasn't in the room.

Outside of the office, the talk grew bolder. At one dinner in the Tap House restaurant in downtown Seattle, where I was with a group of eight young male Microsoft "professionals," including the three from before, the conversation for the full meal revolved around brainstorming ways to seduce her.

I wish I could say that all of this amounted to just talk, but unfortunately it translated into action. Emboldened by the collective group attitude, the single guys would not-so-subtly hit on her, to the point that it was painful to watch. Eventually, the sexual harassment became too much, and Irene left Microsoft *specifically for that reason.* In fact, I personally know about half a dozen women who left Microsoft for similar issues. Sadly, that was most of the women I knew there.

Let me be clear, though: I am not suggesting that my readership should arm themselves with pitchforks and launch a campaign of violence against these supposedly sexist assholes. Rather, I think this behavior stems from a social phenomenon. This phenomenon is that when a large group of people are all doing wrong things and not realizing that what they are doing is wrong, that group becomes self-affirming. What do you think would have happened if in 1930s Germany one Nazi turned to another Nazi and asked, "Hey, is it wrong to hate Jews? Does that make me a bad person?" Well, probably the other Nazi would have said, "Naw, you're overthinking it. Jews are terrible." And the first Nazi would have relaxed, saying something like, "Phew, just needed a reality check. Thanks." I think a similar dynamic is happening broadly in software in the way men treat women.

Unshockingly, software companies are aware of this issue, which has risen to prominence in the industry. One solution has been to simply try and recruit more women. However, the pool of qualified candidates is largely out of their control. Thus, they have taken steps to improve the culture.

Paradoxically, they try to accomplish this by sending women to training and support groups to talk about these struggles and prejudices. From my point of view, this is a super-weird and backward solution, which to me seems akin to hosting therapy sessions for Jews feeling persecuted in a Nazi internment camp, instead of dealing with the Nazis. (If any software HR people in tech are reading this, I highly recommend you start a required course for all male engineers that is taught by an older male engineer voted "least sexist" by the *women* of your company and titled "How Not to Be a Sexist Asshole to Your Female Coworkers." Seriously.)

Anyway, I think that gets the point across that sexism is a problem in the software industry. And I bring this up to highlight how this environmental issue shaped my own actions: I treated women at work with extreme caution. After witnessing how upsetting this environment can be, and watching several female friends depart from the software industry due to it, I was ultrasensitive to the role I play in setting this culture.

So, let me be clear when I say that I was not hitting on Chelsea the Facebook intern. Did I think she was attractive? Yes. Would I have liked to date her? Absolutely. But I made a deliberate effort to keep a lid on it. It's possible that I still made her uncomfortable; I can't rule it out. In fact, I was probably acting like a total loon trying to figure out the balance between being creepy and ignoring her when I joined Armen's team for lunch. But because of this concern, she was definitively in the "people I will never ever, ever, ever consider asking out" category, right up there with family and men.

Fortunately for everyone involved, the summer passed without event. The only thing of note was that Chelsea and I became Facebook friends, as was common among coworkers at Facebook. At some point after the summer ended, Armen mentioned that she had accepted a full-time offer.

Fast-forward to the holidays of 2015. As late December rolled around, I was in a sling due to a climbing accident. But this didn't stop me from flying to my hometown of Seattle to spend Christmas with the family. The Yule time (or is it Yuletide? Maybe it's talking about Christmas- themed laundry detergent ... hmm) was filled with merriment and joy, or at least filled with my brother and I constantly at each other's throats. Ah, family. The best.

Upon my arrival in the Emerald City, I posted a status update to Facebook for people to hit me up. One of the responders was of interest: Chelsea, the former Facebook intern. Obviously, this set off some alarm bells, but I thought to myself, "Hey, there's nothing against getting a drink with a coworker!" We agreed to meet at Gordon Biersch in the Pacific Place mall in Seattle. Given her future position as one of the rare female engineers at Facebook, I decided that it was best to proceed with caution.

When we met at the bar, it was immediately apparent that we got along better than two badgers in a beehive. Within a half hour, what had been a distant we-work-at-the-same-company-and-know-each-other-through-Armen-and-that's-it had developed into a much friendlier rapport. To capitalize on this, I thought it would be fun to show her some of the other bars nearby (when I lived in Seattle my apartment was a mere two blocks from this Gordon Biersch, so I was intimately familiar with the area). After discussing a few options, we settled on Whiskey Bar as our next location, and before you could click your sparkly red heels together, we were off.

At Whiskey Bar, we had a few more drinks. I distinctly remember loving the hot buttered rum and absolutely hating the hot toddy. (I think for her it was the opposite.) In any case, by this point we were getting a bit tipsy and were feeling quite relaxed, and the conversation flowed as easily as the booze.

As the night raced by, Chelsea was sitting next to me at the bar, fiddling with her drink. She looked at me and smiled. "Hey, Colin, did you know that they built a Ferris wheel here in Seattle?"

A wide grin crossed my face and I raised my eyebrows in surprise. "Uh, no, I didn't. Where is it?"

Chelsea said, casually and with authority, smiling softly, "It's just down by the piers. It's really cool."

I swirled my drink a bit, noticing the hint. I tried very hard to play it off like it was no big deal, but I was fighting the alcohol and a smile was slowly winning over my face. "Oh, I didn't know that. Do you want to go?"

Chelsea made no such attempt at subtlety, grinning fully at my response. "Yeah!"

Okay, maybe the exclamation point on the "Yeah" is making her response seem a bit too enthusiastic, but a period sounds so *flat*. Imagine a hybrid punctuation mark between a period and an exclamation point, which means she was willing to ride the Ferris wheel with me, but it's not obvious if that is why she brought it up. (To be clear, I am adding this ambiguity in hindsight. I interpreted it as a suggestion that night.)

And while we're analyzing this situation, I want you to imagine you are alone at a bar on a Saturday night (the day after Christmas, if we want to get technical) with a member of the sex that you are interested in (and that person is also interested in your gender). If that person proposes a Ferris wheel ride alone with you, there is only one thing that you should be thinking right now: FERRIS WHEEL MAKEOUT SESH! I mean, who proposes a platonic Ferris wheel ride while drinking on a Saturday night? No one—that's who.

Given this clearly reasonable viewpoint, I was stoked. This cute, smart, female engineer, whom I got along quite well with, was asking me to join her for a Ferris wheel ride. Best Christmas ever. Given how well I hide my emotions (spoiler alert: I don't), I was nothing short of giddy as we took an Uber to the waterfront and walked up to the ticket counter. I might as well have been shouting to the guy in the booth, who was both underpaid and freezing. "MAN I AM SO EXCITED. SELL ME TWO TICKETS TO STEAMY FERRIS WHEEL MAKEOUT PARADISE. HIGH FIVE, AM I RIGHT?" Boy, I bet if he was single, seeing us must have been rubbing salt in the wound. I do not envy you, ticket man.

Despite my chipper demeanor, Chelsea was disconcertingly quiet while we waited in line for the ride. Maybe my eagerness was giving her pause for thought. Or maybe I had just totally read the situation wrong. Or perhaps the process of sobering up in the cold Seattle air as we waited was clearing her head. I may never know. But what I do know is that she wasn't touching my arm or giving me any clear signal of interest. This didn't mesh well with the one thing that I knew to be true about all people: they don't hide it when they are into you.

To clear up the ambiguity, I devised a test. In a gentlemanly fashion, I would let her into the carriage first and then follow her. But when I sat down, I would make sure we were touching. Not like sitting-on-her-lap touching, just a little too close for friends. The kind of touching that, if she were another straight guy, would cause her to scoot over slightly but not remark on it. The kind of touching that your sibling does when you are forced to share the same bed at a family reunion, and they want you to move over so they can greedily steal more of the sheets (what a jerk!). The kind of touching that, if you were interested in someone, you wouldn't pull away from, but might rather wait and see if they move first. It was the perfect litmus test of attraction.

So with this in mind, I let her into car thirty-seven and sat down. And with no hesitation I say the following: I executed the plan perfectly. She immediately noticed—but much to my dismay, also immediately scooted away. And not in the "you're in my bubble but I still want to be close to you" way; she scooted halfway down the bench. Fortunately, the car had rocked a bit when I stepped on, so it appeared completely accidental on my part. Regardless, the signal had been clear: she deliberately ended contact, by a wide margin.

Disheartened and thrown off my game, my bubbly attitude deflated. While she had been the only quiet one in line, I too was now silent. I sat with my hands folded in my lap, looking out the window on my side so she couldn't see the desolation written across my face. She coughed awkwardly, fidgeting with the edge of her shirt. Her muscles looked tense, as if she were waiting for a job interview. We passed the most uncomfortable Ferris wheel ride of my life in near silence.

Karma must have been at play that night, as when we morosely stepped out of the carriage, the guy who helped us was none other than the lonely ticket taker. I hope that seeing my disheartened face was of sick, cathartic pleasure to him, and that it brought him a glimmer of joy on that coldest of nights. Chelsea and I walked to the exit, where cutesy couples contemplated forking over almost laughable amounts of money for photos of them smooching. It was fortunate that the conversation had died, because otherwise my dour mood would have been evident.

As we stepped toward the street, I waited for the inevitable. "Hey, thanks for coming out with me. I had a lot of fun. See you at work," she would say. We approached the sidewalk. It would be coming in 3 ... 2 ... 1 ...

"Hey, so my brother is having a birthday party tonight in Capitol Hill at my cousin's place. I mean technically it's my aunt and uncle's place but my cousin lives there and they don't. Do you want to come?" Chelsea looked at me expectantly, her face warm and friendly.

I looked back at her skeptically. At this point it was only about 10:00 p.m., and I had nothing better to do. Her invitation seemed genuine. "Uh ... All right. I don't have any other plans this evening." I may have been disheartened by the Ferris wheel ride, but I was not about to throw away the opportunity for at least a friendship. We hopped into the second Uber of the evening and headed over to the party.

We arrived at what I can only describe as the stateliest-looking house in the whole of Seattle, and possibly even the entire West Coast of the United States. The large, U-shaped brick building enclosed a fountained courtyard. Trellises of wood and stone sported twisting ivy which wound all the way up the towering walls. An elaborate steel gate stood before us, topped with fleur-de-lis spikes. If this house had been given a name, it would have been Buck Mulligan. (This is a character in Ulysses; I feel like this should earn me some cred in the writing circles, you know?)

The two of us stepped up to the gate, which had a small callbox affixed to its handle. We pressed the button, but nothing appeared to happen.

"I'll send my brother a text," Chelsea noted, pulling out her phone.

After waiting for a couple of minutes, we tried the gate, but it was indeed locked. There appeared no other entry.

Chelsea tested the firmness of the bars. "We could always just climb over it."

I nodded silently. I was not particularly keen on this approach, as I had only one usable arm because of my recent injury. I technically wasn't even supposed to be out of my sling, but I had felt it would dampen the mood and I left it at home.

Fortunately, Chelsea must have picked up on my reluctance, as she called her brother a few more times instead of hopping the fence. After waiting for a solid ten minutes, Chelsea's cousin, Spike, finally emerged from the front of the house and opened the gate. He led us into the house, where a loud party of roughly twenty people was well under way.

Chelsea's brother, Brandon, came up to join us, and it dawned on me that it must look very much like Chelsea and I were an item at this point. This was not ideal, as both her brother and her cousin must have been at least six foot two and over 180 pounds each. They were also in great shape. Dare I say jacked? I dare. These guys were jacked.

As you might expect, the two of them eyed me suspiciously. They stood close, flexing their burly muscles as they snorted out steam. Spike leaned in close, looking coldly into the whites of my eyes. "So you're here with Chelsea?"

I shrugged, smiling amicably. "Oh yeah, totally. We work together. She's a hoot."

Brandon frowned intensely, glancing over at Spike. "Did you just say Chelsea was 'a hoot'?" He growled as he spoke, fire and brimstone erupting from his gaze.

I punched him in the shoulder playfully. "Ah yeah, man—you know what I mean. She's a blast to hang with." I grinned wickedly at Spike.

The two of them shifted uncomfortably, glancing at each other in confusion. It was as if to say, "Hey, we're big guys, crossing our arms, and getting all up in his space. Shouldn't he be afraid or intimidated or something? Is he that oblivious?"

Of course, I was totally aware that they were trying to pull the classic bad-cop/bad-cop routine, but I would have none of it. The Ferris wheel debacle had made me firmly aware of my place in Chelsea's world (namely, that of a friend) and I would not suffer the grilling of a lover with none of the perks.

Eventually they gave up and the four of us joined the party. In typical tech-city fashion, the party was overwhelmingly dudes. I grabbed a drink and did my best to enjoy myself. Chelsea socialized with her family, and the two of us interacted rather minimally. It was not so much that we weren't on good terms as it was that we had already spent a lot of time with each other in the preceding three hours. I tried to keep a chipper mood, but I was feeling totally crushed, and Chelsea leaving me to my own devices was not helping. Both of us drank heavily.

At around 10:45 p.m., I received a text from an old high school friend of mine, Steven. Both physically and personally, Steven was the mousy male equivalent of Caroline. He was scrawny, with brown hair and an ultra-pale complexion, and he couldn't have come in at more than 140 pounds despite being five foot ten. Relevantly, he was also gay, and, as such, was always hanging out with a posse of his gay friends. Furthermore, I was no stranger to his crew; I had spent a fairly substantial amount of time clubbing with them when I had lived in Seattle. They were at a club just six blocks away. Having not seen him in a substantial amount of time and much desiring to do so, I thought this would be a good opportunity to make an exit and bid Chelsea adieu. I walked over to where she was drinking with her brother.

"Hey, Chelsea, some of my friends are at a nightclub nearby, and I was thinking of heading over to meet up with them." My tone was flat and tired. I didn't smile as I spoke, showcasing a more neutral expression.

Chelsea, who appeared rather bored with her current conversation, brightened up considerably, raising her eyebrows and showing what appeared to be genuine excitement at the prospect. "Oh yeah? That sounds like a lot of fun. I was kind of ready to head out anyway."

My eyes widened. "Oh, so you want to come th—"

Chelsea gave her response even before I finished my question. She smiled widely and her voice was excitedly pitched. "Yeah!"

Let me be clear—the exclamation point very much belongs at the end of this "yeah." Whether her excitement was at the prospect of leaving this party or of hitting the club, I can't say. But whatever her motives, we scurried out of the manor and grabbed our third Uber. And in the Uber, I had a terrifying realization.

I turned to her somewhat sheepishly, my mouth a tense line at not having told her sooner about the nature of our trip. "Hey, just so you know, this is a gay nightclub. These are my gay friends. I'm not gay but they are, and they don't hang out at straight bars. Is that cool with you?"

Chelsea seemed totally unconcerned and continued grinning and looking out the window cheerfully. "Yeah, that should be fine!"

In short order, we rolled up to the club, Diesel. (I have since come to learn that this is what is known as a Bear Bar. I don't know what a "bear" is, but I imagine it's self-descriptive.) I thanked our driver, who winked as she waved us goodbye and wished us luck. Chelsea and I stepped inside the unassuming brick building that housed the club, which was filled with a veritable throng of people. The room boomed with music and conversation, and was packed so full we could hardly get through the front door. We squeezed our way through the crowd as we attempted to search for Steven. We walked the entire floor twice, but my friends were nowhere in sight. Just as I was about to lead us back outside, however, I spotted Steven sitting in a booth in the back corner. I motioned to Chelsea, who was unfortunately wedged between the backs of two large bearded men.

"OH MY GOD IT'S COLIN!" One of Steven's crew, Pierre, jumped up to greet me. He beamed a thousand joys in my direction.

Jake, Pierre's boyfriend, stood up excitedly as well, and we all exchanged hugs and greetings. "It's good to see you again, Colin," remarked Jake.

As we finished our effusive hellos and general banter, everyone made room at the booth for Chelsea and me. Space was at a premium, and the two of us were wedged firmly together at we sat.

Pierre remained standing. "I'm going to get you guys a round of drinks!" He looked over to Chelsea and me, grinning as broadly as any human could. "Vodka Red Bulls?"

"Of course!" I fired back.

"Uhhh, sure," Chelsea said uneasily, frowning slightly and slanting her eyebrows outward. She glanced nervously around the bar.

Within moments of Pierre's departure, I was sharing tales of glory and greatness from the magical land of California. My arrival had placed me nothing shy of the center of attention, and my audience was captivated. The conversation flowed as readily as the vodka Red Bull, and everyone was having a marvelous(ly wasted) time. That is, everyone except Chelsea.

Having been caught in the currents of sociability, I had totally forgotten about Chelsea for at least ten minutes. She hadn't said a word, or even made her presence known during this time. I turned to her, half expecting her to be unhappy or uncomfortable, but her face showed nothing but amazement. I can only speculate that she was shocked that I had so many inroads with this group of people. If you had to ask me what was going through her head, I would say she was mighty impressed.

As I was looking toward her, she took advantage of the lull I had created to put her arm around my waist. Without missing a beat (well, the tempo of the club music was kind of quick so I *might* have missed one), I instinctively put my right arm (the one which I had injured) around her. If my face had been forged into one of excitement and success in line at the Ferris wheel, it had returned in double now. My friends' eyebrows rose slightly as we held each other, but their tongues remained firmly held.

The conversation continued, but I could barely contain the feelin' that had roiled up inside of me. What I had chalked up as a romantic failure had turned out to be a great success. I had shot straight past cloud nine and was blowing through cloud ten. Chelsea had her other hand on my leg now, and after a short bit started tugging at my shirt. I looked down at her and received a hot kiss. What followed was nothing short of an extremely intense makeout session. This was the kind of face mashing that you make some room for because you have a pretty good idea how it's going to end, but you just aren't sure *where*. And while I'm not usually a PDA kind of guy, I wasn't one to turn down a good thing that comes my way.

Our gum swapping continued for a substantial amount of time—at least twenty minutes. When we finally stopped for a break, my friends had cleared out and it was just the two of us in the booth.

Chelsea looked at me expectantly.

I looked back at her, unsure of what exactly the next move was. "What's up, Chelsea?"

She fiddled with the zipper on my jacket, looking down at it. "I was just wondering ... " She stopped for a moment to make eye contact. "If you were into BDSM."

PAUSE. I want you to take this in for a moment. Okay, resume.

My heart skipped a beat, and not in a good way. While I had never done something like this before, I had a strong inclination that it wasn't my cup of tea. But she was such a cool person otherwise, and maybe I would be pleasantly surprised. Roll with it, I thought. "Uh, well, I have never met a girl who was into something like that before. I have never tried it, but I am definitely willing to try anything once."

At this point, I was running logistics through my head. We were both staying with our parents for the holidays. We could go to a hotel? Yeah, that would work. I'll mention that.

"Oh yeah?" A *look* crossed her face. She moved her mouth up to my ear and started to bite me.

Let me be clear what I mean when I say "bite." I don't mean a playful nibble. I don't mean normal sex-level biting. I mean full-on, flesh-rending, Mike Tyson–style ear gnashing. I mean the kind of biting that takes you from relaxed and wasted to a sobering level of alert. I would be lying if I said I didn't recoil.

Despite the van Gogh moment I've just described, I let this happen for a solid few minutes. She didn't literally bite my ear off, thank goodness, but it wasn't for lack of trying. If this wasn't freaking me out enough, she then started pulling my hair. Once more, this was not a playful-tugging kind of pull. This was strong enough that I was seriously concerned about her pulling chunks straight out. In between biting my ears and neck (both very, very hard) she would kiss me on the lips. I distinctly remember tasting the iron flavor of blood and thinking, "Who's bleeding?" and realizing that it was from my ears and neck. I tried to keep my panic to myself. She's just testing the waters, right? I tried to look like I was into it—fake it till you make it.

I reciprocated as best I could, but I was exceedingly troubled by the excruciating pain she was inflicting—and by the fact that she was clearly trying to consume me. Plus, I was hesitant to leave any marks on her in a public bar like this. After all, let's say that a bystander misread the situation and the police showed up, I certainly did not want this to turn around on me. Unfortunately, I think she found my lack of enthusiasm dissatisfying and upped her game. At this point I had hit my limit; the pain was too much. Tears were welling up in my eyes and I couldn't take it.

Using my one good arm to try and gently remove her tugging hand from my scalp, I tried to make eye contact through my wincing. "Can we please stop? This is really hurting me."

She stopped. Her face was as serious as the pale visage of death. It bore neither warmth nor malice. It was forged in resolve. "Look at me," she said.

I looked at her.

She made the most intense eye contact a human has ever made. It went straight through my soul and then came back again just in case it didn't get the point across the first time. "Just accept this. I'm in control."

At this point, I reached full-blown fight-or-flight panic mode. But before I could drunkenly stumble out of the booth and flee, her hand was at my throat.

I now found myself being strangled. For how much alcohol she had, and how petite she was, there was an impressive level of force and coordination coming out of Chelsea. Her right hand held my windpipe like a vice grip. She had me pinned solidly against the back of the booth, and her left hand was once more ripping out my hair. Her teeth sunk firmly into my right ear.

If I could have screamed, I probably would have. But alas, no air could pass, so my face was an expression of mute horror. I snapped into a moment of mental clarity and weighed my options.

"I'm going to be unconscious in around thirty seconds ... maybe a minute?" My eyes scanned for anything that might help. *"Why is no one reacting? Can I get her hand off my neck? If I pass out will she stop?"*

As this raced through my mind, with my one good arm— my weaker left one—I attempted to work her right arm off my neck. It took me an agonizing twenty or thirty seconds, but finally I got her thumb free and liberated myself from her stranglehold. Her drunkenness worked to my advantage, and somehow I got control of both of her wrists. I also must have been shouting "Stop!" repeatedly, because finally she indeed stopped and looked at me with the eyes of someone confused that I was not enjoying myself.

Panting, red-faced, and wide-eyed, I pleaded for mercy. "Chelsea, I'm not just playing. Can you please stop? This really hurts."

The message sunk in, and she seemed to be clear on its implications. Chelsea slumped over a bit and frowned, letting out a long sigh. "I'll call my dad and get a ride home."

The next ten minutes were reminiscent of our ride on the Ferris wheel, except we were both drunker and significantly more uncomfortable. Eventually, her dad showed up and I walked her to the car.

Let's hold up a sec to address the question that many people ask right about now, which is, "Why did no one intervene when I was getting strangled?" I want to immediately dismiss the notion that they didn't notice—the people at the bar weren't blind. They had seen us making out—and her biting me—for the better part of an hour leading up to that. To them, this was probably "our thing," and I don't think they were the kind to judge. To add some credence to that point, my lap and the booth had several condoms on them when I got up to leave. I can only imagine they were thrown at me during the festivities.

In any case, after she departed, I summoned the fourth Uber of the evening and rode home. Fortunately, my family was asleep, and I returned unbothered. It was 1:30 a.m. at this point. Little did I know, however, that my brother had returned home not long before me, when my parents were still awake. Not only that, but he had by coincidence been at the same bar as me that night (he is gay) and witnessed the events I have just described to you. His comment to our mom when he got home? "Colin won't be coming home tonight—he's 'occupied' with a girl." (Thanks for that, bro. Thanks. A. Lot.)

So, you can imagine that my parents were more than a little curious when they found me in the kitchen at 7:00 a.m. the next morning, nursing a very black cup of coffee.

Mom wiped sleep from her eyes as she came down the stairs. "What are you doing up so early, Colin?"

I was wide awake but pretended to be freshly risen as well. "I, uh ... couldn't sleep." I spoke softly, almost hoarsely. My throat had swollen in the night and I had awoken to difficulty breathing. A weak attempt at a yawn made me look even more suspicious.

At this point, Mom noticed my alertness and became considerably alarmed. "You look terrible. What happened?" Dad had also gotten up, and he stepped into the kitchen. As he saw me clearly awake before noon for the first time in his life, he too became concerned. I had washed up the night before, but I still had numerous bruises and scabs on my neck, face, and ears.

He cocked his head slightly as he weighed the situation before him. "Did you get into a bar fight?"

I paused for a moment. Maybe that would be an easier explanation. "Can we get some breakfast and I'll explain it?"

My parents agreed—casting looks of fear at each other at the idea of me *volunteering* to do anything before the sun had risen. We hopped into the family van and drove to the nearby Lumber Mill Café.

During that drive, I had resolved to tell them the truth about what happened. I usually am very private about my romantic life with them, but I figured a bar fight would make me sound like some sort of unsavory ruffian. And so, I told them the whole story—everything I told you now, dear reader—which they listened to in silence. A silence that lasted a full five minutes after I had finished talking.

As we exchanged awkward glances, my mom finally broke the ice. "Wow." My parents both looked as uncomfortable as two humans could. Dad licked his lips nervously and got up to go to the restroom.

That was the only thing they had to say on the matter. They paid up and we drove home wordlessly. When we arrived their awkward energy finally was too much, and they set out to run some errands. We never spoke of it again.

As for Chelsea and me, neither of us texted the other after that. I discovered through colleagues that she took a position in Facebook's New York City office, and I figured that the issue had sort of resolved itself. To this day, I don't have a good plan for if we meet again, but I can promise you that whatever we do won't involve me saying the phrase, "I'll try anything once."

Test Drive

I WANT YOU TO IMAGINE for a moment that you are sitting in a chair. This might not be too difficult, because odds are quite good that you are sitting down right now, and a chair is a reasonable place to be doing such a thing. Except this is one of those cheap plastic folding chairs, and you're sitting in the audience of a crowded bookstore. The chair you are in is in the fourth row, two in from the aisle that partitions the room in half, and you barely have enough legroom to keep your knees from bumping the significantly-too-sweaty older gentleman in front of you (if you are a particularly tall individual, you can imagine that your knees are firmly wedged into the small of his back, making this an uncomfortable situation indeed). Every chair in this overly stuffed room is full, and the edges of the room are lined by standing persons.

An average-height Caucasian man strides out of the back room and up onto the rickety platform at the front of the room with a swagger like no other. His long brown hair glistens beneath the flickering incandescent lighting, perfectly complementing his angular features, pasty skin, and rather pointy nose. He flips his flowing locks majestically, sending waves of "Oooohs" and "Aaaahs" throughout the audience (in case you had not figured it out, this person can only be me). The man steps up to a battered microphone, and after some unpleasant adjustment and feedback from the sound system, he asks the audience:

"How many of you have been on a date that ended in an unexpected manner?"

Nearly the entire room raises their hand, including the speaker.

"And how many of you have been on a hiking date?"

Most of the people who have their hands up put them down. A scattering of hands remains.

"And how many of those hiking dates involved a car accident, during a 'test drive'?"

Everyone puts his or her hand down except the speaker, and a chuckle passes through the room.

"Ah, darn. I always hope that someone else has had that happen! Well, let's begin."

With a premise like this, where exactly to start the story is a difficult question (apparently, I choose the route of a hypothetical bookstore presentation). This tale covers a particularly strange chain of events that occurred during what should have been a rather straightforward date to go on a hike up Mission Peak. I'm going to start from the veeeeeerrrrry beginning, which will lead us down a long and meandering trail toward our eventual plot events. If you find the prospect of such a garden-path journey dreadful, I highly recommend that you use Ctrl+F to find the first instance of the name "Katy" and start there. If you don't happen to be reading this as a bootlegged PDF, then I guess you are just stuck reading the whole thing. Sucks to be you, bro.

Our tale begins where our last chapter left off, in the last few days of 2015. I was burned out. I had been through over seventy first dates. The online dates had failed. Dating my friends had failed. Dating my coworkers had failed, except for Mindy, and that could hardly be counted as a success. I was ready to call it quits. I had stopped using Tinder and OkCupid. Only Coffee Meets Bagel remained. Why I kept using that app I couldn't say. I suspect it was probably because it metered me to swiping on only one person per day, and that felt like a manageable pace.

Despite this relative trickle of possible partners, I still went on a few dates. Enter supporting character one, Joyce. (You know, I've always wanted to introduce someone as a grip, because I see that in movie credits all the time. To this day, I still have no idea what that is, and I would love to meet one.) Joyce was a short Italian girl with a wicked smile and long, straight brown hair. After matching on Coffee Meets Bagel, we decided to meet up for dancing in downtown Mountain View the coming Wednesday.

This was no ordinary dancing, however. This was bachata at Alberto's. Having never heard of bachata, nor Alberto's, I was naturally intrigued and a little nervous. A quick Google search revealed that it was a South American salsa-like concoction. Fortunately, when we arrived at 7:30 p.m., a group beginner lesson was starting, and before we knew it we were movin' and groovin' to the scintillating sounds of a sexy Latin beat. Eh, "movin' and groovin'" might be a stretch. I think it's safe to say that *Joyce* was flowing to the music, but I was more than doubly left-footed. I kept bumping (read as: crashing) us into other people, stepping on her feet, and generally making a scene on the dance floor. On more than one occasion, the instructor, Pantea, had to come over and correct me, as my flailing was growing too painful to watch.

Oddly enough, despite this floundering, the sparks were flying. There was a certain magic that permeated our very beings (along with gobs and gobs of sweat). Time passed slowly and quickly all at once, our hearts interlocked in *la pasión del momento*. The music flowed through us as our bodies swirled in a steamy sound-filled sensation. Our eyes flashed lightning, fire, ice, plasma, and roses as we swept across the dance floor. The night was ours for the taking, and we seized it will all our love, all our sorrow, and all our anger. We were not slaves to the music—the beat came at the beckoning of our own two feet! The sky shook with a furious thunder and the ground wept rivers of joy! Nothing could hold us back! (Except Pantea. She did that a couple of times when we got too rowdy.)

Eventually our corporeal beings could no longer keep up with our burning spirits, and we bounced from the club at around 10:00 p.m. to get some ice cream nearby at Gelato Classico. But when we rolled up, it was nothing short of packed. In addition to having a line out the door, it was filled to the brim with plaques denoting its numerous annual "best ice cream shop in this exact location" awards, and the counter was manned by an old (presumably Italian?) man with a gruff demeanor but a certain unfriendly charm. Unfortunately, his awards were for delicious ice cream and not speed, so the line turned out to be quite a long experience.

Despite having to wait, I was in great spirits. This was the first online date I had had fun on in a long, long while. In fact, it didn't even feel like work! But while waiting in line, an odd thing happened with Joyce: she just casually dropped in the phrase "the country of Hawaii." I can't tell you what we were talking about or how Hawaii even came up, but sure enough it did and she slid that right into the conversation. I almost let it go, thinking she was probably just a bit nervous and her tongue had moved a bit faster than her head. However, I was worried that she was a "birther," and that was DEFINITELY a bomb I wanted to check for before things developed further.

Nervously, I broke the flow of conversation, casting her a worried glance. "Hey, Joyce, you know you just said 'the country of Hawaii,' right?"

Joyce smiled innocently, not acknowledging my concern. "Oh, yeah."

Unsatisfied with her response, I pressed further, frowning slightly and furrowing my brow. "You know it's a state. It's part of the United States. Not its own country. You know that, right?"

Joyce continued smiling. "Yep."

I raised an eyebrow and screwed up my face in confusion. "Ah, so you just said it by accident, then?"

Joyce remained pleasant and unbothered by my apparent concern. "Nope."

I now grew quite flustered, raising my voice slightly. "Why on earth would you intentionally say that Hawaii is a country when you fully know that it isn't?"

Joyce smiled knowingly. "I was just seeing if you were listening."

At this point my heart had come to a complete stop. I think it's fair to say that most dates are a kind of test; you both are trying to figure out if the other person is interesting. But never had I had an *explicit* test, or at least not one so overt.

I looked at her accusingly. "What do you mean you were seeing if I was listening? Is this a date or some kind of trial by fire?"

Joyce chuckled slightly, seemingly unfazed by my frustration. "I have been on a lot of dates where guys would listen and nod, responding with 'oh yes' and 'mhm, that is very interesting.' Their minimal-interaction responses showed that they were just wanting to date Joyce the body [i.e., they wanted to get some] and had little desire to actually interact with Joyce the person."

I took a step back, rubbing my chin with my hand. "So you are saying that by throwing in tidbits like that you can see who is actually paying attention?"

Joyce nodded.

I relaxed, lowering my vocal intensity. "I can understand that. But you do realize I was *this close* to not correcting you, not because I didn't notice, but because I didn't want to be rude. In fact, if the whole Hawaii-is-not-a-state-so-Obama-isn't-from-the-USA thing wasn't a thing I never would have even brought it up, even though I was in fact listening."

Joyce shrugged. "Yeah, I guess that's true."

I frowned sideways, trying to figure out how we could reach an accord. "Okay, well, I have demonstrated that I am listening. Are the tests over? I don't want to be walking on eggshells here trying to catch each little trap you throw into the conversation."

Joyce smiled, changing the topic back to whatever had brought up Hawaii in the first place.

Despite the deliciousness of the ice cream, and otherwise fascinating conversation we had, there were several (and I mean several, not a couple, nor a few) points where I was calling her out on obviously wrong things. Things that I knew she knew better on. (How could I know she knew? You are just going to have to trust me on this. I realize that there is a reasonable chance she was just making mistakes and trying to cover for it, but given the way that she made those mistakes, they seemed completely intentional, possibly even planned.) I couldn't tell if it was just a game or if she was legitimately testing me, but after an hour of intriguing and exhausting discourse we eventually parted ways.

After something like that, you might imagine that I had little interest in seeing her again. After all, I'd had some rough experiences with people who enjoyed messing with my head. But everything else had gone well, and her otherwise consistent and open attitude didn't raise any red flags. I was willing to ascribe that one eccentricity as her method for dealing with the messed-up dating scene in Silicon Valley. I thought to myself, "Hey, let's give this at least one more shot." I texted Joyce the next day and we agreed to a second date.

As fate had it, we went on three more dates. There isn't much to speak of there, other than it ended with her disappointingly taking a pass. However, she learned that I played acoustic guitar, and invited me to join her band. I accepted, as I was on the hunt for such an opportunity and not particularly sore at how things turned out with her.

If this story has acts, this is where we begin Act Two. Please hold for a moment while the stage crew changes props, and feel free to get up and use the restroom. When you get back, we shall begin anew with the introduction of our second supporting character, a man by the name of Richard.

Richard was the Kenny G of the band, the resident clarinet player. He had short dark hair and a quiet, deep voice. He also tended to grin a lot, and had a solidly upbeat and polite demeanor. Recently he had moved from New York (which I continued to refer to as the Promised Land), so I was picking his brain like you wouldn't believe about how good the dating scene was there. We promptly became Facebook friends and decided to go on a hike together.

Our hike went well. Clearly like-minded individuals, we bonded over shared experiences in love and software. Plus, we both liked the outdoors. Damn, why did he have to be a dude? (This is a thought I have way too often. To be perfectly honest, I think that it's a shame that I am straight. Being gay or bisexual would be SO much easier. But I digress.) Given how well our first hike went, we decided another one was in order. A date, a time, and a location was set.

The night before the hike to be—a trip to Sweeney Ridge, about fifteen miles south of San Francisco—Richard informed me that two of his friends would be coming. I didn't think much of it until Richard's Ford Focus pulled into my driveway and contained not one but TWO women. I was shocked. Finding women to go on activities with as a guy in Silicon Valley is about as easy as catching an antelope at a marketing conference—you're completely in the wrong place and will probably look stupid and/or drunk. Most social events are lucky if they can pull a 30/70 ratio, and it's not uncommon to have get-togethers of fifteen or twenty people that are total sausage fests. So, when Richard rolled up with a reverse double ratio, I guess you could say he was my new best friend.

I did my best to conceal my disbelief as I hopped in the car (I may have pinched myself a couple of times, and asked Richard if they were mirages; nothing too awkward). The ladies introduced themselves as Katy and Julia, and they were opposites personality-wise. Katy was very, very quiet, and Julia was very, very loud. Both were what I assume to be average-height South American girls—Katy was from Brazil, but I could not place Julia's ethnic origins confidently. They both had long, straight black hair, although Katy had a much narrower face and more defined chin than Julia, who had a rounder, flatter face with softer features.

The one hitch was that the more gregarious girl, Julia, from pretty much the moment I got into Richard's car, was displeased with the lack of words coming from the quieter Katy, whom she shared the backseat with.

"So, tell us about yourself Katy," Julia said, turning to face Katy head-on.

"Uh ... I'm not really sure what to say." Katie's quiet voice could barely be heard over the road noise.

"Well, you haven't said anything since Richard and I picked you up. Say something!" Julia's voice got more insistent, bordering on outright frustration.

Sitting shotgun, I turned to see Katy shrug, melting into her seat with a look of abject discomfort on her face.

"Fine, if you won't say anything now then you have to say at least one thing for every mile of the hike. Richard, how long is the hike?" Julia demanded.

"Six miles," Richard replied flatly.

Julia crossed her arms. "Six things. Better start thinking."

I turned forward again in my seat, surprised at Julia's brusqueness. On the other hand, Katy's silence was music to my ears. Since many software engineers tend to be hardcore introverts, I had years of experience interacting with these kinds of people. Thus, I was well versed on the nuances of such interactions.

Once we got to the trail and started hiking, Richard and Julia took the lead, and Katy and I took the rear. I waited for the conversation between Richard and Julia to pick up, then dropped Katy and me back a bit so that we could talk more exclusively, mostly to take the pressure of Julia off. I then started asking Katy some basic questions: where was she from, how did she know Richard, what did she do—simple stuff to get her warmed up. No demands or statements about how much she had to say. Fortunately, she was quite amenable to my low-pressure tactics, and we had a nice chat for a solid half of the hike. As we talked, something about her resonated with me. She was rational and critical—having a master's degree in electrical engineering—but still compassionate. I felt energized by her methodical way of looking at the world. Before long, the conversation felt easy, and she was speaking without prompting. By the time the hike finished, we had exchanged numbers.

Okay, so after such a masterful handling of that situation, I better have landed a date with Katy, right? Well, I did. Feeling confident after what I saw as a smashing success on the hike, I took her to the beer hall Gourmet Haus Staudt. It's a nice little beer garden in Redwood City and it has a warm and lively atmosphere. (It's somewhat famous in Silicon Valley because an Apple engineer notoriously left a prototype iPhone there.) It's also one of my favorite places to eat, and I highly recommend it. (Note to the editor: keep track of the endorsements; I'm hoping to make some serious moolah if one of these pays out.)

At the bar, the loud setting contrasted well with our quiet and close conversation. After a couple of drinks, we went back to my place and played some guitar together. At this point, there was no physical romancing to speak of—which was fine, because I felt like we had a chance at something more long-term. If it sounds big of me to say something so thoughtful and mature, you should know that what I am saying is that I asked her for a kiss and she turned me down.

And that pretty much concludes our story. What, you thought there was more? You wanted a car accident? You were misled? I'm a con man, a charlatan? Whoa, whoa, whoa there, buddy, what kind of writer do you take me for? I'm just joshing. Sheesh. Calm down a bit, okay? The best is yet to come! Your patience will pay off, I promise. (Colin's Promises are open to legal residents of the contiguous United States and Canada [excluding Minnesota & Quebec]. You must be eighteen years or older to play. No purchase necessary. Side effects may include disbelief, nausea, sudden limb loss, increased libido, and in rare cases, the growth of a third eye. Consult your doctor to see if Colin's Promises are right for you.)

Okay, so the sparks may not have flown on the first real date, but I was hardly ready to throw in the towel. Deciding to stick with what worked, I thought another hike might win over her guarded heart. I proposed the timeless (and grueling) trail of Mission Peak, the classic San Francisco Bay Area hike. I even offered to pick her up at her house and carry the backpack. And much to my delight, she accepted.

As planned, the following Saturday morning I rolled up to her door at around 10:30 a.m. The trail, 5.6 miles and 2,200 feet in elevation gain, was about a half hour away, and given that we were both in decent shape, I figured we could do the whole thing and be back at her place by around 3:00 p.m. I had in fact been counting on it to keep plans I'd made in the area for 4:00 p.m. I sat in my car and waited for her to come out, glancing up nervously at the sky. It had been raining hard for the previous week, and today was overcast. Unfortunately, I had lost my rain jacket, and the looming threat of precipitation concerned me greatly.

As I scowled at the clouds, Katy piled into my jalopy and we set off. (Can a single person pile into something? How many people does it take to make a pile? Also, to be clear, by "jalopy" I still mean Ford Focus.) Laying the charm on as thick as I could, I offered to buy her a Starbucks on the way. She accepted and we drove to the nearest one. This turned out to be the one just south of Stanford, but as it didn't have a drive-thru we parked and went inside.

As Katy and I stood in line, I surveyed the menu of options, contemplating which combination of adjectives I would throw together to form a sugary caffeine heaven. Katy, however, was glued to her phone. After about a minute, she looked up and asked me tentatively, "Hey I just got a text from a guy I am trying to buy a car from. He says he can bring it by Stanford at 11:00 a.m. Would it be okay if we stopped by so I could look?"

I pulled out my phone. The clock read 10:46 a.m. "Sure, that sounds fine. We aren't in a huge hurry." I wasn't super keen to awkwardly tag along for a used-car examination, but it was a chance to curry favor and I wasn't about to pass that up.

After grabbing our drinks, we drove to the Stanford Oval, a large grassy area surrounded by parking lots and quintessentially Stanford buildings (if you ever see a photo of Stanford, this is probably what you're looking at). We found parking at a little past 11:00 a.m., but even at this late juncture Katy had heard nothing further from the would-be car salesman. We hopped out of my car and decided to walk around. She kindly thought to show me the sights, as this was her alma mater. Not feeling like bringing up my ex, I accepted the tour, even though I had deep familiarity with the school from visiting Stella so much.

After what felt like an eon and a half, the guy we were supposed to meet finally showed up. Or rather, we somehow bumped into his wife at a bus stop, who promptly texted him. It was now 11:45 a.m., and if things didn't progress rapidly this date was in serious risk of smunching into my post-hike plans. The guy, a slim, dark-haired, bushy-eyebrowed microbiology postdoc at a nearby Stanford-affiliated lab, was a serious and stern fellow. His wife, on the other hand, could not have been more the opposite; she was as bubbly and warm as she was blond and Russian (to be clear, she was all of those things). For the life of me I can't remember their names, so we can just call them Gordon and Tanya.

As we met, an intense frown crossed Gordon's face. "You didn't mention that you were bringing your husband." He gestured to me.

"And you didn't mention that you were bringing your wife," Katy retorted, squinting her eyes and nodding toward Tanya.

Tanya and I looked at each other sheepishly. Although I was a little miffed that Katy didn't correct him, I figured this was probably not the best time to mention that I was on a second date and not, in fact, Katy's husband. I turned back to Gordon and smiled.

Gordon didn't acknowledge my warmth. Without changing his expression, he turned away from us and started walking. "Let me show you the car."

After a short jaunt, the four of us stood before a tan 2005 Mazda 3, which was clearly in bad shape, at least cosmetically. Gordon's frown vanished, and he tried his best to strike an upbeat tone. "It may seem like $2,800 is asking a lot given its ... aesthetic condition ... but I assure you that she is mechanically very sound."

Gordon then pointed to the numerous dents and holes in both bumpers, explaining how each one came to be. After detailing the exterior, he opened the doors and showed us the inside, which shockingly was even more dilapidated. The inside door paneling was carpeted, and there was not a single place where that fabric was not at least half peeled off. The seats were stained and torn, badly needing reupholstering. To say that this car looked terrible would be giving it the benefit of the doubt.

Despite what appeared to be a clear nonstarter, Katy asked many questions about the condition of the car and its operations. I was kind of surprised she would even consider buying something that was such an eyesore, but I wasn't about to jump in and say as much—I was her fake husband, remember? And as a good fake husband, I figured my role was to smile, nod, and if prompted, say, "Yes, dear. It's lovely, dear." After all, maybe she was just going through the motions to be polite.

"Can I take it for a test drive?" Katy inquired.

"Well, so much for my theory about her just being polite," I thought.

Gordon furrowed his brow and crossed his arms. "Let's be clear: I'm selling you my heavily used, college beater car. I don't know what you are expecting here."

Katy leaned in ever so slightly toward Gordon, raising her voice and gesturing at the car. "Well, I'm not buying any car that I can't verify at least drives."

Gordon took a step back, rubbing the back of his head. "I see." Gordon looked to his wife, who shrugged, then back to Katy. "Fine. We can take it for a short drive around the block."

With that, Katy hopped into the driver's seat while Tanya and Gordon took the back. I rode shotgun, figuring that after a few laps around the oval we could be done with this and get on with the date. With a flick of the key and a groan of the engine, we were off.

Yet after about three or four minutes I grew concerned. Gordon had made it very clear that he wanted this test drive to be brief, but Katy was decidedly driving somewhere. This kind of thing is hard to tell because the roads around Stanford are windy and confusing, and if you aren't familiar with them it is not always clear which cardinal direction you are going. (This is a subtle Stanford joke; the Stanford football team is called the Cardinals.) To the inexperienced, nearly every path feels like you are going in circles (sounds a lot like my dating life, huh?). However, both Katy and I had spent substantial amounts of time at Stanford, and it was clear to me that we were taking the most direct route to Page Mill Road, which is decidedly how you leave campus. I nervously looked to the backseat to where Gordon and Tanya sat—neither seemed to have the foggiest idea what was going on.

After around five minutes we neared the edge of campus. "Would it be okay if I took it on the freeway to make sure it works at highway speeds?" Katy inquired.

"Ugh. I guess so," Gordon grudgingly conceded.

At this point, I was 100% CERTAIN that Gordon and Tanya were unfamiliar with Stanford's campus (for the record, the bio lab Gordon worked at is not on campus). Anyone who was familiar would know that just getting onto Page Mill Road, at the southeastern border of campus, was a good eight minutes from the oval. From there it takes another seven minutes to get to the nearest freeway, I-280. Counting the drive back, this plan would mean that our trip would take a minimum of thirty minutes. I sincerely doubted the irritable Gordon, who sat with a resting frown and crossed arms, knew what he had just signed up for.

Yet off we were. I figured I had come this far with Katy, and I sure as hell wasn't going to be the one to take the wind out of her sails. Good fake husband, remember? Plus, this would give me an opportunity to see how she handled a tricky situation. As for me, I decided that the most diplomatic route would be to chat with our grumpy host. And without a doubt, what better way to connect with him than over his field of study, microbiology. Of course, I didn't know anything about microbiology, but I like to think I held my own in that conversation reasonably well, all things considered.

While chatting with Gordon, I periodically glanced toward Katy, trying to get her attention. After all, we were supposed to be hiking right now. However, she kept her gaze decidedly forward-focused, and I resolved to address the situation later.

After another few minutes, we turned onto I-280, where we spent the next five minutes driving mostly in silence. Katy noted the fact that the airbag light was on, but this revelation was met by shrugs and incoherent mumbling from the backseat. By now, it had been a solid twenty minutes since we had started driving, and I was kind of wondering how long this was going to keep up. The time must have been about half past noon at this point, and there was no way I was going to be on time to my afternoon event.

Finally, at around the twenty-five-minute mark, Gordon stepped in, shouting, "Where the hell are you taking us? I said you could test-drive for a few minutes around campus, not take us on an hour-long joyride. Take us back right now!" I could see him gesturing forcefully in my peripheral vision.

Katy adjusted her grip uncomfortably on the steering wheel. Her face was forged in a frown. She took a deep breath as she prepared her rebuke. I decided that if there was a time for me to step in, now was it. I pulled out my phone. "I can get us directions back, Katy—take this next exit up here."

Katy let out her breath and nodded wordlessly. Within a minute we got off the freeway at Farm Hill Boulevard. Unfortunately, I had chosen a particularly poor exit, because there is no good place to do a U-turn there. This caused us to get mixed up in some neighborhoods as we tried to figure out how to get back onto I-280 in the other direction. As we drove, Gordon could hardly keep his mouth shut.

"Unbelievable. This is unbelievable. It's been thirty-five minutes. I agree to a short lap around the block, and this is what we get." Gordon's face was red and his voice loud.

Tanya placed a hand on his shoulder, smiling. "You've had a very pleasant conversation with Katy's husband, though, haven't you? You're always saying you want to meet new people."

Gordon quieted, reducing his complaints to incoherent grumbling.

Eventually we got back on Farm Hill Boulevard toward I-280 and saw signs for the on-ramp. Since Katy knew where she was going from here, I turned my eyes to the sky. The looming clouds had kept their peace long enough. It began to rain.

I doubt I will ever discuss such a thing again in my life, but the topography of this on-ramp is particularly important for what happens next. The first thing I should note is that Farm Hill passes directly under the freeway at roughly a ninety-degree angle. As we crossed this point I can only imagine that Katy thought we were already on the on-ramp, because she had begun accelerating to freeway speeds. I'm kind of curious what was running through her mind, because she had to know that she was going to have to make a hard-left turn to get onto the freeway right above us.

The second thing I should note is that our direction on Farm Hill turned into the southbound on-ramp. The other direction was fed by the southbound off-ramp, which meant that the two crisscrossed each other at a T intersection. The off-ramp had a stop sign, but our direction did not.

By the time I looked back at the road from my mindless gazing, we were going about fifty-five miles per hour and were about seventy feet from the T-intersection. In front of us were two cars stopped at the off-ramp sign, one car in the intersection, and a car in our lane that we were rapidly gaining on. I believe this is the point where everyone in the car started to scream.

Given how fast we were going and how hard of a left turn we had to make on wet pavement, I think this reaction was well justified. And as her three passengers started to yell, Katy slammed on the brakes, effectively locking them up. The tires screeched loudly as we skidded across the freshly wet asphalt. Miraculously, the car in the intersection and the one that was in front of us stepped on the gas, and with screeching tires all around, narrowly got out of our way. How they saw (or heard) us in time is a total mystery to me.

Additionally, seventy feet is not a lot for coming to a complete stop in the rain while skidding with your brakes locked at fifty-five miles per hour. In fact, it's completely impossible in a tan 2005 Mazda 3. Fortunately—and I owe the civil engineer of San Mateo County a whole six-pack of beer for this one—a small dirt embankment had been constructed on the leeward side of this intersection, which gracefully absorbed most of our roughly forty-mile-per-hour impact.

Given that before this point I had never been in a high-speed car accident, I think it is fair to assume that most readers have not been in one as well. I'll tell you what it is like. You might expect it to feel terrifying, especially given that everyone is yelling. But it was surprisingly calm. The screams weren't mindless; they consisted of remarkably coherent instructions to Katy. And although it took maybe a second from when we realized what was happening to when we hit the backstop, in the heightened sense of awareness, time seemed to pass much more slowly. I distinctly remember thinking, "Huh—I thought a serious car accident would be more alarming than this" as we were skidding toward certain doom. Very surreal, to be sure.

The collision itself was an explosion of dirt followed by a grinding halt. A few deathly silent seconds passed and we collected ourselves, finding ourselves at a much steeper angle than we had been previously. I looked out the window: we sat perched on top of about half of the dirt pile, the rest of it either on the car, in the car, or scattered around the car. After making sure everyone was all right, we got out to a gathering group of witnesses. Since everyone seemed fine, we told all the looky-loos to mosey along; we could handle this ourselves.

Once it was established that everyone was okay, Gordon turned to me. "Help me push the car down." As he spoke, he was neither angry nor loud, simply very direct and commanding. He pointed me to the mangled front of the car. The two of us walked over, and after about a minute of shoving, we got it onto the shoulder of the road.

Wordlessly, Gordon began inspecting the car. I followed him, noting that the front bumper basically didn't exist anymore—it had been firmly smooshed against the bottom of the car. More precisely, it was in a lot of places a front bumper should not be in. It was in the wheel wells. It was where the now-bent radiator was supposed to be. It was dragging on the ground just in front of the forward axle. It was also dangerously close to touching that axle. To make matters worse, wires were dangling from spots, and I wasn't 100% sure where or what they were originally attached to. To boot, the car was now a filthy mess.

After inspecting the car, Gordon shot straight past mad to irate. He and Katy began an argument while I texted my friends that I would not be making our afternoon plans.

Let's size up the situation for a moment. I was originally going to go hiking with Katy up Mission Peak. Instead, I was standing next to a severely damaged car, in the rain (without a raincoat, remember?), having just been in the accident that severely damaged said car, watching a couple of people I barely knew arguing with each other.

I hopped back into the conversation to find Gordon's fists clenched and his face bright red. He waved his hands in a gesture an umpire would typically use to declare a runner safe. "No. We are NOT calling insurance. Not happening." He paused for a moment, thinking. "You know what, why don't we use your insurance?"

Katy crossed her arms, glaring at Gordon. "I don't have any because I don't have a car. Besides, I want to call yours because I want an estimate before we go to a mechanic."

Tanya, who had been standing off to the side, literally stepped in. "Katy, it's off the table." Her voice was noticeably calmer than Gordon's, but no less firm.

At this point I realized that neither party had insurance.

Gordon put his fingertips to his now-closed eyes, rubbing them in circles. Suddenly, he stopped, his voice lowering substantially in volume and his tone warming up. He turned to face me. "If you two buy the car and get us a cab back to Stanford, then we can just pretend this whole thing didn't happen."

I looked back at Gordon, perplexed. My mind thought through his words slowly. You TWO? Oh, that's right. They think we're married. Shit. I didn't say anything, but instead looked toward Katy.

"I'm not buying the car until a mechanic looks at it." Katy spoke with force, her tone flat. I wondered for a moment why she would even entertain such an idea. There was a pause in the conversation. It dawned on all of us that we had no way to get to a mechanic, or back to Stanford for that matter. And it was still raining.

Gordon shook his head as he looked from Katy to the car. "Let's see if it starts." He took the keys from Katy and got into the driver's seat. As the rest of us tried to comprehend what he was doing, the car started. Gordon gave it a little gas and the car lurched forward a few feet, accompanied by an awful grinding sound.

"I think the bumper is dragging, Gordon." It was the first thing I had said since noting that I was not injured. Gordon weighed the words and looked under the car. Sure enough, it was.

He popped the trunk and pulled out a bag of zip ties. (WHO KEEPS ZIP TIES IN THEIR TRUNK? What is he, a serial killer?)

Gordon looked at me expectantly. "Let's get to work."

Gordon and I spent the next five minutes fastening the bumper to the underside of the car as best we could. We got the dragging wires and pieces of metal and plastic off the ground, even if just by a centimeter in many places. It was enough to get the car moving.

Gordon drove forward about fifty feet, and tried to turn left and right. The car seemed to turn left well enough, but when Gordon tried to turn right it made a noise like squealing rubber.

"What is that? That sounded like a tire," Gordon remarked. He got out, and with the other two looked at the right wheel well, but there was no apparent source of the problem.

I kneeled, peering into the opposite wheel well. "I think it's coming from the left wheel here." I stood up, facing Gordon.

Gordon continued inspecting the right tire, replying shortly, "It happens when we turn right ... "

I sighed loudly, furrowing my brow. "Gordon, just look."

Gordon came over while Tanya took the steering wheel. She turned it straight and then right. When she turned right, the front left tire ran into a large protrusion of the bumper and rubbed against it something fierce.

I spoke to Gordon again. "I guess we can't turn right."

"Appears that way," Gordon replied dryly.

As Tanya climbed back out of the car, the three of us looked at Gordon expectantly. Would we be calling in a tow, then?

"Let's go." Gordon climbed into the driver's seat. His wife took shotgun without a word. Katy hesitated and looked at me, but I just pretended not to notice and got into the backseat. She reluctantly followed. In case you had forgotten, we were on the on-ramp to the freeway, so there was only one-way to go: onto I-280. It was still raining.

Hold up. Let's rewind a second here. Every time I tell this story, people ask me, "Once the accident happened, why didn't you just say, 'Fuck this. I'm not Katy's husband; I'm just some rando on a date with her and we were supposed to go hiking. I'm not even sure how the hell I got into this mess. I'm so out.' Then you could have hopped in an Uber and gotten the heck away from there, never to see any of them again." I wish I could say why I didn't do that. I wish I *knew* why I didn't do that.

If I had to guess, I think the reason is that I felt bad for Katy. She already was doing a top-notch job of convincing Gordon and Tanya that she was unreasonable. If I had said who I was and left, I suspect they would have gone nuts on her.

So here we were back on I-280, now headed to Stanford, with the capability to make exactly zero right turns in a car held together by zip ties and hope. Despite a situation that should have certainly ended in our deaths, somehow the drive went miraculously well, save for the fact that Katy and Gordon wasted no time continuing their argument.

"Are you sure the brakes worked properly?" Katy quizzed.

Gordon turned around in the driver's seat, clenching his teeth. "Are you kidding me? Of course the brakes worked properly. I can't believe you're even asking." Even the good-natured Tanya was now squeezing her fists.

"It seemed like they locked up. Good brakes would've stopped a lot quicker," Katy replied coldly.

Gordon and Tanya looked at each other intensely, veins popping in their necks.

I interjected. "Look, Katy, there are no brakes on earth that could have saved you from that accident. You can't take a sharp left turn with seventy feet of wet road at fifty-five miles per hour. Period."

The car immediately went silent. Gordon and Tanya looked at each other again, something close to a pleasant expression crossing their faces. I hazard to guess that they were surprised to see me taking their side (probably because they thought Katy and I shared a bank account). Katy said nothing in response. I can only imagine that she was thanking her stars that I had not explained the true nature of my involvement or simply left.

The rest of our trip was one of the tensest car rides of my life. (Right up there with the time one of my girlfriends mistakenly thought she was pregnant and told me on the way to McDonald's at 2:00 a.m. Yeah, that was a fun couple of weeks.) Eventually we got back to the Stanford Oval in one zip-tied piece. Gordon and Tanya dropped Katy and me off at my car and told us to meet them at a nearby mechanic, which happened to be the only one open on this Saturday. I reluctantly agreed.

As you can imagine, sitting alone with Katy in my car was an uncomfortable experience. I said nothing, hoping to make the drive in silence. Katy took this opportunity to inform me that the Kelly Blue Book value on the Mazda was not more than $2,000 and that $2,800 was asking too much. Plus, she was sure that the car was totaled, so she wasn't going to buy it anyway. *"There is going to be an interesting conversation at the mechanic's,"* I thought.

If the time to leave was way, way, way before this point, this was nothing short of a perfect opportunity for me to make a significantly belated departure from the scene. I could have dropped Katy off at the mechanic's, bid her adieu, and been home with the whole afternoon ahead of me. However, I had come this far and I wanted to see it through. Katy needed a ride home anyway, and I wasn't about to abandon her. Despite her surly demeanor toward Gordon, she seemed a bit in over her head; I know I would have been had the roles been reversed. I also thought the situation would benefit from a calm presence. So, I parked my car and we walked up to the mechanic's shop, a little attachment onto a Shell station, just as Gordon and Tanya were pulling in.

The mechanic came over, took the keys, and had Gordon and Tanya fill out some paperwork. Within a minute or two, the two of them came over to talk to Katy and me. Having had fifteen minutes to cool off, they were considerably more amicable than when we had left them. However, within about five seconds that all changed. (I'm not even sure how it happened, and I was there the whole time!) Before you could say, "The quick brown fox was feeling kind of tired and decided to go around the dog this time," Katy and Gordon were at it again.

After a few minutes of heated exchange, Gordon had had enough. He walked over to me. "Colin, can we work this out? Just you and me?" He cast a sidelong glance at Katy.

I looked over to Katy, avoiding eye contact with Gordon. "Um. No, I really think Katy should handle this."

Gordon spoke calmly, his voice even and measured. "Look, Colin. I think this would get resolved a lot more coolly and satisfactorily for everyone involved if you and me handled this."

Tanya jumped in, nodding her head vigorously. "Oh yes. I agree."

I continued looking to Katy, who stood by frowning with her arms crossed. "Katy, why don't you come over and settle this with Gordon? I am going to run into the gas station and grab a soda." Before Gordon could get a word in edgewise, I turned on my heels and hightailed it into the mini-mart.

"Mini-mart" is absolutely the wrong word for this market. Even micro-mart would be generous. Probably the best unit of measurement for measuring this place would have been the number of atoms across. I seriously doubt I could've lay down diagonally.

Despite the market's having 50% of its volume occupied by the clerk and another 85% of its volume occupied by merchandise, I was in no hurry to leave. It was kind of awkward because all I could do was turn in circles and look at the same fifty-odd items repeatedly. I did this for about ten minutes. (The guy at the counter asked me at one point what the heck I was doing, and I told him that my wife was outside and I was trying to lay low. He thought this was hilarious. I figured I might as well get some mileage out this fake marriage, right?)

Eventually, enough time had passed and I felt reasonably confident that the matter was resolved. Or at the very least, that one of the parties would be a pile of meat, destroyed by the fury of the other. I came out to thankfully find that the first possibility was true, and Katy signaled that it was time to go. I offered a ride to the now-carless Gordon and Tanya, but they politely declined. Despite my relatively nonexistent contributions, they thanked me for being calm. We shook hands. I think I would have gotten along with them rather swimmingly had we met under better circumstances!

As Katy and I hopped into my car, I checked my clock. It was now almost 2:00 p.m. and we were both thoroughly exhausted. I was also famished. I turned to Katy. "Hey, do you want to get some food? I'm really hungry."

Katy raised her eyebrows and looked at me skeptically. I think she was surprised that I was willing to spend more time with her. "Uh, yeah. What did you have in mind?"

"Bagels," I said, totally unemotionally.

"Bagels?" she questioned.

"Bagels," I replied flatly.

Katy lowered her eyebrows, frowning ever so slightly. "Uh, okay."

We drove to one of my favorite bagel places, Izzy's Bagels, just down the road.

As we ate, Katy scrunched her mouth to the side. "So, yeah. Sorry about that. I feel pretty embarrassed about the whole thing."

I glanced up from my bagel momentarily to make eye contact. For a moment I considered asking her how the whole thing had resolved, but I decided to wait. "It happens, Katy. I'm not going to hold it against you for getting in a car accident."

Katy nodded, noting my sincerity. "Yeah. Still, I'm guessing you are probably going to be dropping me off after this, though?"

I looked back at her blankly. I took another bite of bagel, chewed, and looked out the window at the passing pedestrians. A small child in coveralls and bright yellow rain boots was poking at a wet leaf with a stick. "Well, I don't really have any plans for today. I was going to meet some friends after the hike, but I told them I wasn't going to make it after we got into the crash. My day is kind of dead at this point. Honestly, I still want to go hiking. Do you want to come?"

Katy smiled. "Sure."

It was settled. Three hours and one car accident later, the hike was still on. After finishing our food, we got into my car and drove to Mission Peak.

Finally, a full four hours after we had first left her house, we got to the trailhead and miraculously snagged the best spot in the otherwise full lot. By now it had stopped raining, which was good because I still didn't have a jacket. The two of us hit the trail.

Due to the volume of rain in the preceding week and hours, the trail was not so much a trail as it was a muddy slip-and-slide. The unfortunately high clay content in the soil made the path particularly treacherous. Nothing crazy happened, other than we made it to the top, cut it uncomfortably close to the park closing, and got totally covered in mud from slipping and falling while hurrying back. (Well, I did at least. I don't think Katy fell at all.) We got back to my car just as the sun was dipping below the horizon. We were both exhausted physically, emotionally, and mentally. Despite the events of the day, I still had had a reasonably good time. Maybe Katy wasn't half bad.

I don't know if you are a hiker, dear reader, but the car ride back from a hiking trip or any long outdoor activity that involves significant exertion is usually very quiet. This was no exception.

Eventually, I broke the silence, speaking softly as we drove toward the setting sun. "Hey, so, do you want to grab some Taco Bell drive-thru on the way home? I'm feeling pretty hungry after all that hiking." I looked to Katy.

Katy continued staring fixedly at the road in front of us. "No, could you please just take me back to my place?"

I nodded. "Yeah, okay."

She turned to me. "So I just want you to know, I'm not ... " She looked back at the road, screwing up her face as she struggled for words.

My tone was flat. "Interested?"

"Yeah," Katy noted, relieved.

I stared ahead at the road, frowning. "Gotcha."

This revelation sparked a mix of emotions in me. On the one hand, she was under no obligation to keep dating me if she wasn't feeling it. After all, the whole point of dating is to feel these things out. But at the same time, I felt seriously annoyed. After all, I had done her a tremendous solid that day. In fact, I had done her like ten solids back to back. It seemed like rubbing salt in the wound to say something like that so soon after the fact. This was a pretty rough ending to a very rough day. But at least I hadn't crashed someone's car.

After everything that transpired, you might think that I didn't see Katy again. At the very least you might expect that Richard, who had introduced me to Katy, got an earful. Neither of these things was true. In fact, I don't think Richard even knows that any of this took place. And he probably won't find out until he reads this book! (And then he'll be all like, "Awwwww whaaaat? That's CRAZY.") Regardless, the next time I went to play with the band, to my surprise, Katy was there. It turned out she was a pretty good drummer, and we *needed* a drummer. And that's pretty much how things have been ever since.

I do like to use this story, though, as a cautionary tale to guys moving to Silicon Valley: this is the only place on earth where you can have a girl drag you through such an incredibly disastrous date and still have her be the one to break it off at the end. I wish I could say that this kind of behavior was atypical, but I can't tell you how many times I have gone on "dates" where girls tried to get away with ridiculous things like dragging me on a used-car test drive. I can only imagine that they do this because they know that they have the power by being such a rare commodity. And while some women go the route of Joyce and try and filter out the guys who are willing to put up with it, other women have no issue taking full advantage.

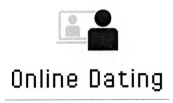

Online Dating

F I HAD BEEN BURNED OUT on dating before, by the time Valentine's Day 2016 rolled around, I was completely done. I could hardly believe how many dates I had been on, and I simply wanted to call it quits. What could another dozen or so first dates hope to offer other than more suffering?

At this point, you might be thinking, "Colin, surely *you* must be the problem if after eighty-four first dates you haven't been able to find someone!" Now hold on just one moment there. First, I had only been on eighty first dates by Valentine's Day (great counterargument, no?). Second, it wasn't like all eighty of them had turned me down (even I am not that unlovable). Rather, no one had wanted to keep dating me while I also wanted to keep dating them. This was at least partially because I didn't want to settle. Remember that previously I had gone to the effort of applying to every English-speaking game studio of over one hundred employees to become a game designer—a job that I could leave or change at any time? Why would I not put in at least that much effort when searching for a *permanent* life partner? I wasn't just looking to get laid, or just looking for a girlfriend: I was looking for that special someone. And finding her was proving to be surprisingly challenging.

The day after Valentine's Day, I lamented my situation to my coworkers over lunch. As we sat on plush ottomans around a trendy (read as: overdesigned) and completely useless coffee-table-stool thing, I spun a tale of woe and despair. "I just don't see the point in trying anymore," I said, sagging my face into my hands in desolation. "I mean, unless I leave for the Promised Land, there is no hope that I will ever find love."

Tessa, the product manager on my team, spoke up, giving me a stern and highly skeptical glance. "Maybe you need to try something different. I'm sure the location is not the problem."

Joseph, the master coffee-smith you might remember from the introduction, jokingly offered a solution in his typically amicable manner. "You could always use your Facebook ad credits for dating."

Everyone at the table chuckled. Everyone except my manager, Eric.

Now, Eric is normally a jovial and outspoken guy. However, he had sat quietly and listened to this conversation. As the laughter died down, his face became very serious. "You know, that might actually work."

Everyone looked at him quizzically. We were all thinking the same thing: *"Is he serious?"*

Okay, let's time-out for a second. For those who aren't familiar with Facebook's employee perks, one of them is that all full-time employees get $250 per month in ad credits to use on Facebook. And for those outside of tech, ad credits might seem like an odd perk to give out. After all, what is a normal person going to do with ad money? The answer is simple: not much. In fact, the ad credit "perk" isn't a perk at all. Rather, it's given out for dogfooding purposes. (Dogfooding is when a company tests out products on employees first to catch issues before a wider rollout.) This means it is given out pretty much entirely for the purposes of testing and feedback. Since there isn't a good personal use for these credits, the company widely encourages employees to use them to help charities and small businesses, although this is more of a guideline than a hard-and-fast rule. The only hard restrictions are that you must make and run the ads yourself (otherwise it's not dogfooding) and you can't make money off the ads you run. After accounting for these restrictions, it's probably not surprising that most Facebookers outside of the ads team don't use these credits.

Anyway, getting back to the lunch conversation, the table was silent as everyone weighed the idea of using monthly ad credits to promote me for dating. I was the first to break the silence, speaking in a somewhat doubtful tone. "But aren't there restrictions on how I can use these credits? I mean, that kind of constitutes a conflict of interest, right?"

Eric shook his head. "I'm pretty sure the policy states that unless you're doing something that makes you money, you're in the clear. We can check it out after lunch."

Tessa's eyes lit up. "Oh my god, we could get someone from the design team to make Colin an ad!"

I scratched my chin. My mind was reeling with questions and ideas. "But I only get $250 a month ... I mean that's hardly enough to reach a sizable audience ... right?"

My coworkers didn't miss a beat. Coffee-master Joseph was the first to speak, his eyes alight with excitement. "I would absolutely throw in my $250 a month for this."

Tessa chimed in as well. "Yeah, I'm in too."

A couple more teammates, Peter and Shay, also excitedly threw their hats into the ring. "Count us in!"

I nodded my head, a wide grin crossing my face. "If this is allowed ... then with this kind of money, I could reach thousands, maybe tens of thousands of people!"

The table became a buzz of discussion. Ideas flew this way and that. Could we use the carousel ads? What about look-alike groups? What kind of call to action should we use? Thoughts about how to execute such an ad campaign bubbled nonstop for another fifteen minutes.

After lunch ended, I raced back to my desk and pulled up the employee ad dogfooding policy. I read through it a dozen times. Everything looked fine, except for one particularly vague clause. It stated that an employee could not gain implicitly or explicitly using ads, except with a business that had less than $5,000 in annual revenue. What exactly did "implicit gain" mean? I wasn't making any money off the ads—did that mean I was in the clear? If anything, dates cost me money, so that would constitute negative gain, right? I did a quick search in an online legal dictionary, but the picture wasn't any clearer. I ran over to Joseph, who sat next to Eric, and had him pull up the policy while the three of us read it over.

Once we finished, Eric and Joseph looked at each other and shrugged. Eric placed a hand on my shoulder and calmly smiled. "I think that clause is mostly to prevent people from taking advantage of the dogfooding program for monetary gain. You're probably in the clear."

I raised a concerned eyebrow, turning from the computer screen to Eric. "What do you mean 'probably'? I don't want to risk losing my job."

Eric waved dismissively. "You're totally fine. Dating ads are not the kind of thing that they are worried about. Worst-case scenario: they change the policy and tell you to stop."

I nodded enthusiastically. "Yeah, all right then. Let's do this!"

Now, even though I had the blessing of my manager and wasn't violating any policies, at this point you might be wondering why on earth I would do something so crazy as to run a dating ad for myself on Facebook. After all, wouldn't this just end up as a huge embarrassment?

The short answer is yes; it *could* end up as a huge embarrassment. However, "could" and "would" are very different words. And I saw Facebook dating ads not as a risk but as an opportunity.

First, I knew that using ads for dating was not a new idea. As late as the 1990s, people could take out personal ads in newspapers when looking for love (and for all I know you still can today). Now, I had absolutely no idea what kind of people these were—maybe personal ads were highly stigmatized and only total weirdos did it— but I was willing to bet it wasn't a huge deal and most of the people were normal. Thus, I wasn't worried about the dating ads causing me social embarrassment. Who cares if my friends know I'm single and looking? Not me.

Second, I spent a lot of time looking at how many female users there were on online dating sites like OkCupid and Tinder versus the population as a whole. I'll spare you the boring details, but in the end, I could *prove* that a large percentage of single women in their twenties had no presence on dating apps. (By my estimation around 40 to 65% of young single women were not online dating.)

Yet one app was on every millennial's phone. Okay, that's not true, but this app is really, REALLY popular. It's far more popular than Tinder or OkCupid. You know what app that is? Facebook. And

Facebook is a platform that allows you to advertise to people using obscenely specific metrics. Only want to target girls who like green Reeboks and listen to The Clash? Boom, Facebook ads targeting has you covered.

Suddenly, it dawned on me that there was a massive pool of single women on Facebook who weren't on dating sites. Furthermore, I could target those women using tools that allowed far more specificity than any dating site did. And if that wasn't good enough, on online dating sites I was just another fish in a sea of fish. In fact, one app is literally called Plenty of Fish. I didn't want to be in a sea with plenty of fish—I wanted to be the only fish! The last thing my dating life needed was for me to be pictured right next to a six-foot-two brain surgeon with rippling abs. If that guy was a marlin, then I was a flounder.

But on Facebook, most ads were typically promoting normal things, like armchairs. People see armchairs every day on Facebook. But what they don't see are fish. On Facebook, I was going to be a fish in a sea of armchairs. Women would see me and be all like, "Whoa, what is this ad for a fish doing here? I'm going to click on this because it's so new and surprising!" Jackpot.

Emboldened by this clearly sound reasoning and by the fact that I wasn't technically doing anything wrong, I immediately went to work setting up an ad campaign. Of course, the implementation would turn out to be harder than the idea itself (isn't it always?), and there were some hitches right from the get-go. First, you couldn't advertise personal Facebook pages, so I had to make a public figure page. I wasn't exactly a public figure, but this made the most sense to me. I made my "call to action" a link to my OkCupid account, so that people would have an anonymous way to contact me. I filled the page with details and photos. But I kept the tag line simple: "Message Colin now to set up a date!"

Another hitch was that I had no likes. And let's be honest, no one goes on a date with a zero-likes guy. That guy is just weird. If I was going to do this, I needed a fan base. So, what did I do? I invited all 806 of my Facebook friends to like my dating page. (For anyone else considering this, learn from my mistakes and don't invite your parents. Or grandparents ...)

For the ads themselves, I set up a campaign targeting women 21–29 years old (+/- 4 years from my age of 25). I also only targeted women with a "single" or "unspecified" relationship status who had at least a bachelor's degree. I set my region to within a few miles of Menlo Park, where I worked and lived. For ad content, I wanted something that captured my charming and quirky personality. I chose the following:

I hit the "publish" button and my ads were off and running! Well, more accurately, they had to be approved first, but after a few hours they were off! Now all I needed was to scale up my operation. To do this, I first turned to my immediate team. Their having enthusiastically pledged their undying support at our lunch/brainstorming session, I expected nothing shy of full cooperation. What I found was quite the opposite.

I engaged Tessa and Shay first, as they sat next to each other and were the first two people I saw after setting up the page. I strolled over to their desks, filled with enthusiasm. "Hey, guys, ready to set up that ad campaign?"

The duo exchanged sheepish looks. "I think I'm going to pass," Tessa said dismissively.

I turned to Shay, my face filled with surprise and confusion. She frowned and looked to the side. "Am I going to get fired for this?"

I scratched my head, thoroughly confused. "Why would you get fired?"

Shay looked down at the floor, nervously playing with a pen. "I don't know, I mean we work for Facebook. Should we really do something like this?"

I looked back at her dumbfounded. "I don't understand. It's not like we are abusing any special employee powers that let us do things normal people can't. The whole point of the dogfooding program is to simulate what it's like to be a normal ads user. Anyone could do this exact thing if they wanted. We just happen to have $250 a month burning a hole in our pockets that we can only use on Facebook ads. Why on earth would we be fired for doing the thing this program is literally designed for—testing ads in new ways?"

Shay shrugged, biting hard on her lower lip. "What if the media picks up on it?"

I laughed. "Man, the media picks up on *everything* we do. If I bought a house and posted a pic on Facebook, I'd more likely than not end up on the front page of a newspaper with a title like 'Facebook employee gentrifies unsuspecting neighborhood, also murders kittens with pitchfork.' I'm not going to live my life afraid of someone misinterpreting my completely legitimate actions." I beamed confidently at Shay, defiant in my self-righteousness.

It's important to note at this point that I do not have a quiet voice, and this rousing speech carried quite a distance through the open office space. I like to imagine that it did a lot to sway my other team members in earshot.

Shay capitulated, and within a few days I had a half-dozen people at Oculus supporting my cause. Since virtually no one had run ads before, I had to teach them how to use Facebook's ad tools, as well as provide them with photos. I quickly realized that this was not scalable. I knew that I could disseminate this information more easily through a Facebook group, so I set one up named "Colin's Love Quest." I uploaded a selection of several photos and provided all the targeting information people would need.

By the end of the first week, I realized that I would need more than six people involved to get this ball truly rolling. I posted a thread in the Oculus employee forum requesting people to contribute their unused ad credits. I expected to be ridiculed, or maybe even outright told to stop, but instead I received a wave of supportive responses and another four advertisers.

Around this time, my initial target population—about 64,000 women living in Silicon Valley—had started responding to my ads. My page crossed a hundred likes, and one thousand people had clicked on my ad. But more important, I'd received about ten messages, all of which were from women who were genuinely interested in going on a date with me. I had expected at least a little backlash, but everyone who responded to my page was both supportive and excited. I cleared my calendar for the next month.

Despite having several inquirers, I still didn't have an *actual* date lined up. I suspected that this was at least partially because only a fraction of the single women in Silicon Valley were seeing my ads. This view was augmented by the fact that Tessa and Shay—both committed to a man but listed on Facebook as "Unspecified"—were in the target group but had not seen my ad even once. The only explanation I could come up with was that I had too little money to reach everyone. Thus, I decided it was time to up my ad credit recruitment game. I went around Oculus and asked everyone I knew to help me out.

Many people were reluctant at first, but once I hit around twenty contributing employees, my ad campaign started to take off. The buzz this generated around the office pushed several previously hesitant people to participate. Even Tessa and Joseph, who had been decidedly out at the beginning, jumped on board. Tessa ran a rather intriguing ad:

By the end of week two, I had over thirty advertisers coordinating through Colin's Love Quest. More people were starting ad campaigns than I knew what to do with. Both Tessa and Shay had gone from not seeing my ads at all to seeing them *several times per day*. I needed to branch out farther. I sent out a message to the entire group to increase the ad radius—we needed to target the entire San Francisco Bay Area.

My target population was now well over 100,000 women. But since more of my coworkers had started contributing ad credits,

Tessa and Shay still saw three ads per day. I have no idea if this was true of every woman in the San Francisco Bay Area, but what I do know is that every woman in their twenties that I already knew was now sending me texts. "Why on earth am I seeing an ad to date you in my news feed?" one asked. "And why am seeing it multiple times per day!?" By the third week of the campaign, over 12,000 people were visiting my page on a weekly basis. I was gaining around a hundred likes per week, and that number was steadily climbing.

As the third week continued, I realized that I had forgotten one of the first rules of online dating—there is usually a two-week lag between swiping on people and getting responses. I was finding that Facebook ads were no different. My inbox was getting dozens and dozens of interested messages per day—I literally couldn't keep up with the rate people were reaching out to me. (Despite this, I still managed to earn a 100% response rate and seven-minute average response time badge on my page!) For the first time in my adult dating life, I was the one getting flooded with messages and not the one doing the flooding. It was everything I had hoped online dating could be.

More important, I realized that the users of Facebook were capable of something amazing. In all the responses, not one was negative. Not one. People called me "brave" and "funny" and "cute" (actually, they said the dog in my ad was cute, but that's beside the point). I had expected at least one person to find the ads distasteful. Heck, I had expected it to blow up like a YouTube comment section. Yet what I got was a sea of posts spilling over with amusement, interest, and compassion.

Paradoxically, by the time the fourth week started, I had only been on four first dates. Setting them up had been straightforward as I already had a game plan: take them to bubble tea places in their part of town. But getting interested ladies to *commit* to plans was turning out to be more challenging than I expected, as they naturally were hesitant to go on a date with a guy from a Facebook ad. I wasn't too worried, though—the floodgates had only just been opened.

However, everything changed when a member of the Facebook security team reached out to me. He had heard through the grapevine that other Facebook people were unhappy. Policy people. They had taken notice of my campaign and were planning to put a stop to it. And within minutes of my receiving his message, something far more concerning happened—a reporter sent me a text message.

Let's go into the backstory behind this text message. By the time I started these ads, my roommates Marion and Vicky had had enough of my shenanigans and decided they wanted out of our house. (In reality, Vicky wanted to move to San Francisco and Marion wanted to save cash and move in with her parents.) In the last week we lived together, Vicky went out drinking with her soon-to-be new roommates. While out, Vicky checked her Facebook page and saw one of my ads. Naturally she freaked out, thinking that someone was playing a joke on me. When she got home, I explained to her what I was doing, and in the week that followed, she evidently shared this information with her new roommates. One of them happened to be a reporter. This reporter friend-of-a-friend was intrigued and wanted to set up an interview with me.

Realizing that this situation was heating up, I decided to play it safe and reach out to the ads policy team proactively, just to make sure I was on the up-and-up. I also emailed the press team at Facebook to let them know about the reporter's inquiries. The next day, Facebook decided to put a stop to my ad campaign.

That said, the shutdown of my operation was quite professional. First, the ads team decided that this use of advertising credit didn't constitute dogfooding, and I was politely asked to stop running the page, which I did. I also did an interview with the reporter through the Facebook press team, which turned out to be far less exciting than the reporter had hoped. Anticipating drama, the press team had carefully coached me on what to say and what questions I could and could not answer, and the result was so milquetoast boring that I doubt it will ever make it to print. Even if it does, I hardly expect it will be the sensational article my teammates feared.

In the end, I learned a lot. First, the dating campaign cost a lot less than you might think—the final value came to around $63 per initial contact. If we further assume that this could be broadly applied to every single guy out there (let me be blunt: you probably can't; I don't think this will scale), this would mean that for about $1,000 you can get sixteen women to reach out to you in one of the most difficult dating scenes in the country—all for relatively minimal effort. That's not bad!

Yet despite having dozens of people respond to my ad, I only went on those four first dates. I wish I could say that there was a good reason for that, but it was mostly because I was still burned out from all of the online dating. Oddly enough, those were the four best first dates I'd been on since I moved to Silicon Valley. All four women were fascinating individuals, and it was somewhat heartbreaking for me that none of them wanted to date me long-term (to be fair, in one case it was mutual, after she repeatedly asked to bring knives into my bedroom for some fear-factor foreplay. I adamantly declined).

Despite not finding "Miss Right" and ultimately getting shut down by my employer, I would consider this experiment a resounding success. I had more people reaching out to me for dates through Facebook ads than through any other platform I had tried. I reached people who had previously been unreachable due to a lack of presence in conventional dating apps. I also found a relatively easy way to turn money into dates, which is something I couldn't do before! And if nothing else, the 100% positive written feedback I received was both highly surprising and encouraging. Even the people saying, "Don't give up—I know how hard it can be. I'm pulling for you," made it all worthwhile. And while I won't be trying this stunt again anytime soon, I certainly hope I won't be the last person to advertise for dating on Facebook.

The J. J. Abrams of Book Endings

WELL, THAT'S ALL I GOT. And given what I'd experienced up until this point, you might imagine that I've become quite the wizened old sage. Envision tattered brown robes hanging over my bowed shoulders. Perhaps a flowing white beard now garbs my gaunt cheekbones. Leathery skin falls in thick folds around my joints, and a quiet, raspy voice warns younger men of the dangers of dating in the West. (For this illustration, please also imagine me clutching a gnarled staff.)

Okay, so that might be putting it a bit dramatically. But you are probably still wondering how everything turned out. Am I still single? Did I move to New York City? Have I gone on more dates? Will anyone use my Jaipur set?!

The answer to these burning questions and more will be provided in book two: *The Promised Land*. Preorders available now!

Nah, I'm just pulling your leg. As it turns out, I did leave Oculus for the East Coast (although not the Promised Land, sadly!). Tired of striking out, I decided to trade romantic for intellectual fulfillment, and I'm now working on a master's in Applied Physics at Cornell, which leaves me still single, and still looking for love. In the end, everything ended up in much the same place it started.

But after going through these crazy experiences, all in the name or romance, *something* must have changed, right? After all, no sane human being can go through such an ordeal and not learn something. Well, I did learn something. But I think for you to properly understand my lessons you need to know something more about Facebook as a place to work.

If you have never been to the Facebook campus—which is probably the case for most people in the world—it's nothing short of a modern marvel. Many people compare it to Disneyland. In fact, the campus was supposedly designed with help from two Disney consultants. In addition to being beautiful, it has doctors, a barber, a bank, free food, ice cream, and virtually everything else you could want. But during my first two weeks at Facebook, I was focused mostly on figuring out how to do my job. About this time, my manager, Eric, came over to check up on me.

"Getting settled in, Colin?" Eric smiled as he surveyed my new computer equipment.

"Yeah, I think so!" I replied, nodding vigorously.

"That's great!" Eric picked up a plastic dinosaur from my desk, raising an eyebrow as he inspected it. "Enjoying the campus amenities? Have you been to Philz yet?"

I scrunched my face in confusion as I looked back at Eric. "I don't even know what 'Philz' is."

"WHAT?!" Eric threw his hands into the air as he shouted, tossing my plastic dinosaur halfway across the room and into an unsuspecting cup of coffee with a splash. I jolted back in my chair in surprise at his sudden outburst, nearly falling out. He gestured frantically for me to get up. "We must go at once!"

Now, for those not from Northern California, Philz is a local coffee chain that only serves premium coffee. Legend has it that when Facebook contracted them to come to campus, Facebook offered to pay for all the coffee, making it one of the free services. However, Phil himself defiantly stated, "My coffee is so good, people will pay for it!" Indeed, the line at Philz is often quite long, even though the coffee costs actual money, which is remarkable given that there are dozens of free espresso machines littering the campus.

Free or not, I wasn't one to argue, and our walk over to Philz was as pleasant as could be. The trees and flowers were in spring bloom, and the sun shone warmly on this seventy-degree day. We stepped into the aromatic coffee shop, and immediately I was overwhelmed by a myriad of menu options with titles like "Philtered Soul" and "Tesora," coffee names which resembled none I had ever seen before.

The girl at the counter greeted me with a pleasant smile and a soft voice. "Hi there. What can I get you?"

I looked up at the impossibly large selection, utterly overwhelmed. I stuttered a stock response. "Um, can I just get a mocha?"

The girl was now preparing someone else's drink while talking and responded in as friendly a manner as before, "We don't have mochas."

I nodded absentmindedly, still staring blankly at the massive wall of text before me. "Oh, okay. A latte then."

The girl raised her eyes, casting me a look of mild disbelief. "We don't have those either."

I looked back at her quizzically. "Um, what *do* you have?"

The girl gestured at the board, smiling broadly. "Everything you see here!"

Eric jumped in, making a wide sweeping gesturing with his hands. "We'll both have large Mint Mojitos, sweet and creamy!"

The girl nodded and began preparing the drinks. Eric and I walked to the register, and before I could even grab my wallet he had already paid.

"Don't worry about it." He waved dismissively, in as effusive a manner as one could do.

After chatting for a minute while we waited for the barista to finish, we grabbed our drinks and hustled out of the coffee shop, as Eric had to get to a meeting. As we stepped outside, I took my first sip of this Mint Mojito—Philz's signature drink—and was immediately in love. (For the record, "love" is no exaggeration here! I would get one every day for the next six months after that. But eventually I left Miss Mojito for Lady Tesora.)

I distinctly remember thinking, as I sipped my coffee in the sunny Facebook paradise, that I wouldn't change a thing in my life. Just two weeks prior I had moved to the same city as my longtime girlfriend Stella and started my dream job, working in virtual reality at the preeminent company in the field, the Oculus division of Facebook. The sun was literally shining, the birds were figuratively shining, and I was feeling shiny too. My life was amazing.

A month later, Stella dumped me.

As I sat there drowning in the news, I could barely choke out the words. "I moved here for you," I gasped between sobs. "This is the life I want to live. Just a few weeks ago I thought, 'This is perfect. I wouldn't change a thing.'"

Stella listened to those stuttered words, sighing exasperatedly as I finished. She looked out her window and crossed her arms. "That's the thing: it's so hard to stay at that perfect place in life. It's this ephemeral thing I constantly feel like I'm chasing and can never get ahold of."

I blurted my response loudly and pitifully. "But we had it!"

She bristled, casting me a glare. "*You* had it, and only briefly."

Seven months later, I would be sitting in a doctor's office for the third time that winter, being told that I had herpes and that the only plausible explanation for why it wasn't going away was that something must be wrong with my immune system. Romantically, I was alone. I had just been ghosted by my not-even girlfriend Mindy, to whom I was playing second-string boyfriend. I was exhausted from the better part of a hundred first dates. I could see little hope in having a family, especially with my new health condition. My roommates and close friends Vicky and Marion would be moving out—I would need to find a new place to live soon. At least I had my fabulous job, but even that was no guarantee. My annual performance review a few weeks earlier had been less than stellar. It felt like everything I treasured was slipping out my grasp.

But as I saw everything falling apart around me, I asked myself something: "Why do I care so much about dating? Or really, any of this?"

I mean, seriously, why was it so important? So what if I stayed single forever? Why did I have to find a girlfriend to be happy? I mean, clearly, I had gotten over my dream of being a game designer. What made love so special?

And as I thought more and more about this, I wondered something else. When I left Rockstar Games, how much did my absence slow down their development? Probably not much. And realistically, how much worse is their next massive title going to be because I am not there? Probably not much worse. Heck, I was just using Rockstar as a stepping-stone to becoming the supposed "J. J. Abrams of Game

Design," a mythical and indispensable future figure who somehow redefines expectations in such a way as to be irreplaceable.

Furthermore, if I had died on that perfect day at Philz, at that very second, Oculus and Facebook would have kept operating at the same capacity as if I were still alive. They certainly haven't stopped operating since I left. Hell, even if the entire executive team suddenly keeled over and died, Oculus would probably be fine. Sure, some projects might miss a deadline or two, but I seriously doubt they couldn't pull over a few execs from the rest of Facebook in a relatively short period. In fact, ignoring my immediate friends and family, who *needed* me to be around at all?

And as I thought these terrifying thoughts, I realized that something had subtly changed during the time I had gone from being a kid to becoming an adult. Something had snuck up on me, and I hadn't seen it coming. This thing was that when I was a kid, I didn't need to have a purpose. My purpose was to pay attention in school and grow up so that I could do "amazing things" later. Sure, those "things" were never clearly defined, but that was a problem that adult Colin could solve. Basically, my role in the universe was simply to age. I did that automatically every day by not dying. But once I became an adult, that stopped being true. It happened without event, and without fanfare. Suddenly and silently, I couldn't fall back on the "Oh, I'm just a kid and I don't need to worry about it" argument. And worse yet, every day I spent not figuring this out was one day closer to not ever getting a chance to do whatever those "things" were supposed to be. The clock was no longer validating my existence; it was judging every second I spent not realizing what mattered. Hell, I didn't even know if such a higher calling existed for me. Was I on a fool's errand? Did I have a reason to wake up?

From that dark, dark place, it became clear why I had wanted to have a fulfilling romantic relationship so badly. It wasn't to provide me with a guaranteed bubble tea buddy. It wasn't so I could have someone to vacation to Bolivia with. And it certainly wasn't to have someone with whom I could argue about Scrabble rulings. It was so that I could be an indispensable part of someone's life. It was so that I could be the J. J. Abrams to someone's *Star Wars*, saving the day after Jar Jar had run amok. If I filled that role for someone, even just acceptably, I would be providing a service that could not easily be replaced. I would have a reason to get up every morning, and that reason was that if I didn't, her life would be worse off because of it. By my finding this person, my life would be imbued with meaning.

But even as I realized why I cared so much about finding love, another thought crossed my mind. I had lost my girlfriend of four years right after I moved to be with her. I'd genuinely thought she was the one. Heck, if on the day she broke up with me she had instead asked me to marry her, I would have said yes, no questions asked. And yet, just a short time later, I was already on the hunt for someone else. After all, I had debunked the idea of a soulmate—so why would my place in a woman's life be different? Clearly, that role was not as irreplaceable as I had thought.

Huh.

When I had this final realization, I did the only thing I knew to do in these kinds of deeply stressful situations. I went to Taco Bell. I got a large Mountain Dew, a Crunchwrap Supreme and two crunchy beef tacos, and sat outside and ate them as I watched cars file in and out of the IKEA across the street.

And as I sat there, clogging my arteries at a junky plastic picnic table and feeling existentially pointless, I thought for a moment that a significant percentage of people in Silicon Valley would never even find one loving partner, let alone a replacement for one they lost, simply due to skewed gender ratios. I had known this fact for well over a year. And my answer to this problem, then and now, was simple. If there aren't enough women to go around here, move somewhere else. You think there are women in New York City? Well then, move to New York City. And if you are wrong pick a different city. And if that city is wrong pick another one. Worst-case scenario, you keep picking cities until you succeed or die.

Because at the end of the day, even if there is no guarantee that you will succeed, what better option do you have? Sit around and stress-eat Taco Bell? Keep beating your head against the wall that is the messed-up dating scene of Silicon Valley? I'll pass on those options, thanks.

And I realized that even if I didn't have a purpose right now, there was a clear solution to that as well: I'd go out and find one. Since it's apparently so important to me that I be the J. J. Abrams of *something*, I better try something *really hard* until I either become that or realize it's the wrong thing and try something else. Sure, there is no guarantee that I will find what I am looking for, but then again, there was no guarantee that I was going to find love either, and that wasn't stopping me before. Besides, since when was life in the business of making guarantees? Never, that's when. And better yet, while I'm out there trying to J. J. Abramify whatever crazy thing I think is going to be my next life goal, if I am so very, very lucky, I might just find someone to make that journey with. Or I might get herpes. Sometimes you get that too.

Secret Bonus Chapter A:
Date by Numbers

ENTER SCENE (VIA PULLEY AND ANGELIC MUSIC) Jonathan Soma. Jonathan Soma is ... actually I have no idea who he is. I'm not even sure he knows who he is. Do any of us know who we are? Wow, this is not going in a good direction. Anyway, what I do know is that he doesn't know me and I just name-dropped the shit out of him. If you are reading this, Jon—can I call you Jon?—sorry if this is kind of weird. Also, I'm totally talking to you through a book. Kind of cool, right?

Antics aside, Mr. Soma published an interactive singles map of the USA that I was introduced to around the time I first found myself single as an adult in Seattle. This is a map that shows you the gender ratios of single people in various cities around the country, split up by age groups. It allows you to answer questions like, "What is the ratio of single twenty-something men to single twenty-something women in San Francisco?" The data come from the 2012 American Community Survey, which is run by the U.S. Census Bureau.[1]

Built to visualize demographic data for sexually frustrated folks such as myself, it offered a relatively complete answer to why twenty-something-year-old Colin could not get a good date: there are a ton of dudes on the West Coast.

Unfortunately, digitally interactive maps don't exactly work in books, so I'll distill the big takeaways for you. (If you want you can look up the map yourself and follow along on your computer. Google "Singles Map USA.")

The first major takeaway is that if you look at metro areas of population 750k or greater and narrow it to the 20–29 age group, 100% of cities have more unmarried men than unmarried women. This means that as of 2012, every major city in America has more single young men than single young women. I want to let that sink in for a moment.

"But, Colin!" you reply. "That doesn't make any sense. How can there be more men than women across the entire country? Doesn't it have to even out?"

Well, first, there's not more men than women. In fact, it's quite the opposite. There are more *women* overall in the USA. But it turns out the birth rate is about 107 males to 100 females,[2] which is why there are more men in the younger age groups. It may sound impossible that there are more women than men when male birth rates are higher, but it makes sense once you realize that the life expectancy of the average woman is much higher than that of the average man.

1 Jonathan Soma. The New, Interactive Singles Map. Source: United States Census Bureau. 2012 American Community Survey. Table B12002, Sex By Marital Status by Age for the Population 15 Years and Over (3-Year Estimates). Web. 3 June 2016.

2 "Field Listing, Sex Ratio." *The World Factbook.* United States. Central Intelligence Agency. Web. 3 June 2016.

I like to imagine this is due to the fact that dudes are good at killing themselves doing stupid shenanigans ("Hold my beer, I want to try something ... ")

Another trend one can gather from these data is that women tend to be concentrated on the East Coast, whereas men tend to be concentrated on the West Coast. To give you a rough idea of the magnitude of this effect, there are more surplus single men by about a factor of 2.5 west of the Mississippi relative to east of it. (This is ignoring Florida, which is a male holdout if for no other reason than because it's the most phallically shaped state.)

But while these data give us a rough idea of gender distributions, it does have some limitations.[3] The most important one is that this is "single" as defined on a census form—meaning "single" includes people who are in committed relationships or are engaged. It turns out that of these people, about 26% of them are in committed relationships or engaged.[4]

To see why this matters, let's look at Los Angeles. For people in their twenties, L.A. has a ratio of 16% more single men than women, making it the most female-populated city on the West Coast. But now let's remove 26% of the population to account for people in monogamous heterosexual relationships, taking pairs evenly from men and women. This causes the ratio to jump from a male surplus of 16% to a male surplus of 21%.[5] Yikes.

The reason the effective ratio gets worse is because people typically pair in 1:1 relationships, which means that you are pulling out a greater percentage of women than men. To illustrate this concept,

---

3 One of them is that they don't distinguish heterosexuals from homosexuals. It turns out this doesn't matter for ratios, though, because the rates of homosexuality are the same between genders.

4 Madden, Mary, and Raine, Lee. "Romance In America." *Pew Internet.* Pew Research Center. 13 Feb. 2006. Web. 3 June 2016.

5 I whipped this little statistic up myself using some masterful Excel-fu. Hi-yah!

imagine you have 10 blue marbles and 5 pink marbles. If you remove 4 marbles from each color to simulate 1:1 matches, you end up with 6 blue marbles and only 1 pink marble. By doing this, the ratio of blue marbles to pink marbles went from 2:1 to 6:1. This same thing is happening in West Coast cities with young singles.

It turns out this effect gets more powerful if the ratios start more imbalanced, such as in every other major city on the West Coast. Remember how L.A. went from 16% more men to 21%? Well, San Jose, one of the "manliest" cities in the USA and the unofficial capital of Silicon Valley, goes from 32% more men to 45% more men, since the few women there are even more disproportionately removed by 1:1 pairings than in Los Angeles. I'm sure there is a mathematical name for this, but since I like to use colored marbles as my example I call it *the blue balls effect.*

If this effect isn't bad enough, I want you to now consider the impact of neighboring age groups on the dating pool. What I mean by this is that the 20–29 age group does not exist in a vacuum; someone who is 29 might date someone who is 30, for example. Sadly, the exact amount of crossover is not something I could put a hard number to. However, I will assert that this crossover makes dating even worse for guys in their twenties on the West Coast and slightly better for guys in their twenties on the East Coast.

If you are curious as to why I am making this assertion, I want to note another phenomenon that is shown in Mr. Soma's interactive map: in West Coast cities, there are MORE extra men in the 30–39 age group than in the 20–29 group. By contrast, across the rest of the USA, the ratios shift toward more women. In fact, in many Southern and East Coast cities, single women in their thirties outnumber single men in their thirties.

Let's see an example of this. First we have the West Coast city of Seattle, at 20% more single men than single women in the 20–29 age group. Next we have Atlanta, at 11% more single men than single women in that same age group. Seattle is worse, but by less than a factor of two in terms of surplus dudes. However, in the 30–39 age group, Seattle barely improves to a surplus of 17% single men (one of the only West Coast cities not to worsen), and Atlanta flips to having 7% surplus single *women* in that same band. If you were to compare every major West Coast city with (nearly)[6] every major East Coast city, you would see a similar trend.

Now, you might be thinking, "Colin, I see what you are getting at, but how does this affect singles in their twenties, like you?"

Thanks for asking, dear reader! I would love to explain. Let's go back to Atlanta. As I said before, there are more single women in their thirties than single men. Women in their thirties can and do (although infrequently) date men in their twenties, which means slightly better odds for the rest of the twenty-something single guys. (My parents, by the way, did this very thing. My dad was twenty-nine and my mom was thirty-one when they got married.) Additionally, since Atlanta has an abundance of women in their thirties, Atlanta men in their thirties are more likely to date within their age bracket than to date younger women as they normally would.[7]

I suspect this to be a very powerful effect, and if I had city-specific data on husband-wife age deltas I would expect to see more older women dating younger men in Atlanta than in Seattle, for this very reason. Basically, what I am saying is that a bunch of desperate older dudes on the West Coast are robbing the cradle because

---

6 Excluding all cities in Florida. There are just so many dudes there.

7 On average, husbands are 2.3 years older than their wives. Source: Chalabi, Mona. "What's The Average Age Difference in a Couple?" *FiveThirtyEight.* 22 Jan. 2015. Web. 3 June 2016.

they can't get some with women their own age, and this makes my already difficult task of finding a date even more difficult.

If we want to generalize this idea, we can postulate the following hypothesis: favorable ratios in neighboring age groups improve dating prospects in your age group, and poor neighboring ratios result in an effectively worse ratio in your group due to people "reaching across" groups to satisfy their needs. I don't know what the social science community refers to this phenomenon as, but personally I like to call it the *reach-down hypothesis,* mostly to highlight that older men on the West Coast are reaching down and taking all the young women (jerks!).

Okay, so this looks bad, but I'm still not done. The singles data is stale—four years old as of writing—and thus it's not up to date with the fact that even more men have moved to West Coast cities, leading to worse ratios in 2016 than in 2012. The reason is that tech companies have about a 70% male workforce and are dominant in places like Seattle and Silicon Valley.[8] The ratio is worse if you only look at technical roles in those tech companies, which are a staggering 85% male. Even worserer, the technical jobs in these companies are located primarily on the West Coast, whereas most remote offices are usually in sales or support (meaning the West coast has disproportionately more men relative to overall tech employment ratios). This means that as technology companies hire more and more in these concentrated West Coast locales, it drives the male surplus ratios up further. In case your eyes glazed over with all this statistical mumbo-jumbo, the bottom line is this: *there are a lot more dudes in Seattle and Silicon Valley in 2016 than in 2012 because the tech industry is growing.*

---

8 Cheng, Roger. "Women in Tech: The Numbers Don't Add Up." *CNET.* 6 May 2015. Web. 3 June 2016.

Whew. That was a lot of analysis. Is it ... over? NO! One more nail to put in this coffin. In addition to general age considerations (divide your age by two, add seven—safe lower boundary), I prefer to date people in the same life phase as me. This means that since I am an adult professional, I don't like to date ladies still working through their undergraduate degree on a standard 18–22-year-old post–high school track who live at their parents' place over breaks.

"Why not?" you ask. "You could totally date them!"

You're right. I could.

The reason I don't is that as a financially independent adult, I find it hard to relate to someone who hasn't had to support herself yet. I feel like I have grown up more since I left college than in the preceding ten years combined. College is a bubble, and until you know what it means to be alone in the world with no cafeterias or dorms, facing the inky black void of waking up every day to a nine-to-five job that stretches to infinity, you haven't grown up. Plus, college students often prefer to date other students, so they aren't as accessible. This creates what I call the *mid-twenties dip*, where men in their mid-twenties should expect a dip in dating prospects because mid-twenties women are dating older men (2.3 years older, on average) and women in college are either difficult to access or not in a similar enough life phase to make a suitable partner.

Okay, now I'm done. If I didn't get the point across, basically what I am saying is that the West Coast of the USA today is basically a perfect storm of factors for breeding single, desperate, and lonely twenty-five-year-old men. Conversely, easterly cities like Memphis and New York have the exact same problem for women in their forties and fifties, except it only gets worse as they get older, unlike for men.

So, if you are a twenty-something male looking to not be single for the next ten or twenty years, I highly recommend not moving to the West Coast. If you are already there—leave. There is no hope for you. To be fair, it's not amazing for us anywhere, but it's a hell of a lot better in cities like New York, Atlanta, and Memphis than it is in Seattle and San Jose.

By the way, if you are a single woman and feel the same problem I am describing now and you live in Memphis, New York, or one of these other woman-centric cities, know that your feelings are totally validated by cold, hard data. Your Promised Land lies west, in the Mediterranean coastal climates of California or the rainy darkness of Seattle.

Data aside, I want to highlight one more meaningful takeaway from all of this. For everyone still looking to find love, take note of this fact: no dating sites or advice columns will say it, but where you live has an inordinate impact on your ability to date. Supply-and-demand economics applies just as much to dating as it does to every other market, and it needs to be respected for the powerful effect it can have. Want my advice? Pick a city with a desirable ratio. Buy a poster of it. Hang it up over your bed. Every night before you go to sleep, gingerly touch it. A slow tear might run down your cheek— that's okay, let it happen. Whisper the name of the city as you drift to sleep. Someday, you will reach your Promised Land.

Secret Bonus Chapter B:
One Weird Trick

SYNECDOCHE. IT IS AN INTERESTING WORD, is it not? Try saying it fifteen times as fast as you can, out loud. I don't care if you're on a crowded bus or in a quiet room with a sleeping lover. Just do it. If you really must avoid making a scene, an audible whisper will do. Once you do it, read the next paragraph.

I bet you're expecting some interesting point on psychology, some clever way this ties into an overarching theme. There is no such revelation—I'm just trolling you. I bet you looked silly just now, saying "synecdoche" all those times. The person across from you on the bus is probably giving you a weird look. Heh, you totally fell for it too.

All right, now that I have thoroughly grumpified you, it's time to get to the real point of this appendix: to share some thoughts I have about how to date online. Why am I including such a well-covered topic, one that has literally hundreds of books already devoted to it, in this one? Well, I think I have some insights into the process that other people aren't highlighting. Plus, I promise to make it entertaining. Still not sold? Eh, whatever. You don't have to read it. That's why they call it an appendix.

First, let's look at the established literature. When you examine what most people are saying on the topic of dating optimization, you realize that there is an abundance of advice that flows like the following: be yourself, take showers, get a job, brush your teeth, get into shape, participate in activities, blah, blah, blah. It mostly centers on self-improvement, confidence building, and becoming a better person. I am sure it is effective if done well, but let's be honest—it's a lot of work!

More important, these would-be gurus confuse two totally separate things and treat them as if they were the same. These two things are how good you and your assets are, and how you approach the process of dating. By you and your assets, I mean your face, your body, your personality, your dating profiles, and your photos. If you need help with those, you can get all the info you need with a quick Google search. What I want to address is how you approach dating.

First, I want you to do to me a favor: write down one sentence that says what you want out of dating. If you don't have a piece of paper, just text it to yourself on your phone. The important thing here is to be honest—you are the only one who will see this. (Well, unless people read your texts. You shouldn't let them do that, though.) I'll do it with you. Here are some sample ideas:

- To get laid, as much as possible with as many people as possible.

- To find a steady girlfriend or boyfriend.

- To date someone hotter than my arch-nemesis's significant other, to make myself feel good.

What I wrote down for myself was the following: "To find a woman to spend the rest of my life with." If I could elaborate further, I would probably add some clauses about kids and Bolivia and Pokémon, but that's really not important for now.

What is important, however, is that you are honest about this one thing with yourself. You know why? Because if you don't have a clear goal in mind, how can you even know if you've found what you were looking for when you have found it? You must know what your target is before you can start; otherwise you won't know when to stop.

If your answer, by the way, is "casual sex" and you are a guy, just know that you won't have an easy time of it. It takes a huge amount of commitment in the gym to get yourself to where you need to be to pull that off. Plus, you need to have a GREAT-looking face. I hate to break it to you, but if you are reading this book hoping to figure out how to make it work, you are already probably doomed to failure by genetics. Welcome to the club.

Now that you have a goal in mind, let's dispel the notion that dating *should* be fun. A lot of people acknowledge that dating isn't fun, but most people I talk to feel like it isn't because they are going about it the wrong way. Realistically, this is a process that will feel more like a chore or a part-time job. It will suck. You will feel jaded and hurt at times. At my peak, I was devoting multiple hours per day to dating apps, which netted me around four or five dates a week. That is a grueling pace that I would recommend to no one, but it illustrates my point: dating is hard work. (By the way, this kind of pace is not normal. You don't need to go into insanity mode like I did. But what you should know is that time and energy in reflects dates out.) Oh, and I wouldn't get too discouraged by the fact that other people might have more success than you with less effort. They might just be better looking than you. Try not to sweat it too much.

Since we are on the topic of managing expectations, let's cover another important thing in this area: photos. This is the one thing that EVERYONE in the advice community gets wrong. This blows my mind, considering that literally every advice column, dating blog, and book spends oodles of time talking about photos. What lighting should you use? (Golden hour—one hour before sunset.) What kind of camera? (SLR.) What kinds of people should be in the photos with you? (Attractive opposite gender, ugly same gender.) So on and so forth. These articles tout statistics, which show just how much more attention people get when they use a photo with these magical properties. To prove it, they show the transformative power of replacing a "normal" iPhone mirror selfie with a high-quality professional creation. It's like it's a photo of a whole different person!

You know what I think you should do? Do the opposite. Pick a so-so photo of yourself, in meh lighting. And for the love of god, don't touch it up.

"Are you kidding me, Colin?" you retort. "Why would I sandbag myself like that?"

Easy there, let me explain. Yes, it's true that with what I'm proposing, you are literally guaranteed to get fewer dates with less attractive people. This is a good thing, and I am going to tell you a little story to explain why.

Some time ago, I matched with a girl named Vanessa on Tinder. She had one super-cute headshot, but concerningly, all the other photos were either at a distance or didn't show her face. However, the photos were of her doing cool activities—namely rock climbing and hiking—and I thought that she was trying to showcase her athleticism. This was early on in my dating, so no alarm bells went off.

We chatted briefly, exchanged numbers, and then planned a place and time to meet.

When we met, she was so different looking that I literally did not recognize her when she introduced herself, despite having seen a shoulders-up mug shot. I don't mean different in a good way—I mean worse. Her complexion was very rough compared to her silky-smooth photo. Her face shape didn't match her photo at all. In fact, I would hardly have guessed they were the same ethnicity, let alone the same person. The whole date I couldn't get over how gypped I felt, and it was a flop. What's more telling, though, is that she wanted a second date, and I didn't. What did I tell her?

"I'm not interested, but thanks."

Not much to that response, is there? We'll come back to that.

After the date, I took a second look at her close-up. I immediately noticed the artifacts of Photoshop, which is the kind of thing I now look for. More important, though, remember how I talked about before-and-after photos looking like completely different people? Well, remember that when you show up at the coffee shop, only one of those two people is going to be sitting across from your date.

The take-home here is that you don't want to be a Vanessa, where your date feels cheated. Let me be crystal clear on this point: if you look any degree worse in person than in your photo, LITERALLY NO ONE is going to be happy about that when they meet you. Every single person will feel some degree of disappointment, and more important they won't tell you that *that* is why they don't want a second date. Rather, you will get a generic dismissive reply like, "I'm not interested, but thanks." That is, if you get any reply at all.

The harsh reality of the world is, you are only as good looking as you are. (Deep, right?) Yes, that can change over time, but your photo should accurately reflect how you look when the person who is going to meet you sees you for the first time. Hell, maybe the photo could even be slightly worse. Can you imagine how excited someone is going to be if you are better looking in person?

Plus, at the end of the day, if you were borderline in the photo, showing up worse is not going to do you any favors. Getting a date with someone who would have swiped "No" if they knew what you looked like is just wasting everyone's time. Trust me, they won't change their mind when they experience your "dazzling personality."

If you don't think this is important or common, for me personally this is the number one reason I turn people down for second dates, or simply don't ask for one. People are really, really good at smoothing out their flaws in photos, even you. Sadly, this is (in my opinion) probably the easiest and most painful thing you can do to make your dating life more frustrating. If you take nothing else from this appendix, take away that you should showcase yourself realistically. Yes, you will get fewer dates, but the dates you will be cutting out will be with people it wouldn't have worked with anyway.

Now that we have photos out of the way, let's answer a question that is burning in no one's mind: how do I track my dates? I use a spreadsheet, of course! It is literally a workbook full of women. If I printed it out (it fits neatly on two sheets) and hole-punched it, I could have a binder nowhere near full of women. Kind of disappointing, really.

You might wonder how I reconcile all this cold-blooded "let me consult my spreadsheet" stuff with the desire to find true love, have kids, etc. They don't seem to go with one another, do they? Well, remember how we wrote down a one-sentence goal? I want to accomplish that goal. And I can't imagine a more logical and earnest way of approaching the problem than through careful statistical analysis. Plus, I'm fantastic at using Excel to improve my life. If

I have one strength, it is that. And if I am not going to be hunky or charming, then why would I handicap myself by not fully utilizing my one leg up over the competition? That would be stupid.

More to the point, after going on all these dates and keeping them in Excel, you naturally might wonder what kind of interesting things I have learned. Let's start with some statistics on my success rates. I track the following:

- **Match Rate:** The rate at which women match me per "Yes" swipe. (Not applicable on OkCupid.)

- **Message Rate:** The rate at which women respond if I initiate contact. (Not applicable if they message first.) This also varies a lot based on source, but is around 30% on OkCupid and 50% elsewhere. Forty percent is a good average.

- **Phone Rate:** The rate at which women give me their number after we engage in messaging. I would estimate this holds at a steady 50% across all apps.

- **Date Rate (This really needs a new name. It sounds awful.):** The rate of women I physically see in person after getting their number. I would estimate this at 50%.

- **Sexy Time Rate:** I was going to leave this out, but I know people would notice its absence. This is the rate that I go from date to sex. I personally don't track it, as I am looking for real relationships and not just one-night stands. No judgment from me if this is your jam.

If you multiply these together (ignoring the Sexy Time Rate), this is what I call the Investment Rate, or the rate at which you go from expressing interest to an actual date. For me this comes out to about 1.5% over all the apps (which is kind of meaningless, given the high variance across apps), which means that I need to swipe "Yes" on sixty-seven people to get a date, assuming that I diligently follow through on all of them. The rate is substantially better on OkCupid and Coffee Meets Bagel, probably coming out to around 1 in 20 and 1 in 10, respectively, from interest to date, and substantially worse on Tinder, coming out to fewer than 1 in 200.

Even if these data are flawed and I am a terrible, terrible data scientist, one thing that helps about having these numbers in mind is that it keeps things in perspective. It's very easy to get attached to a person you match with and feel excited about. But if you treat everyone as a statistic until you meet them in person, it helps soften the blow of the losses and temper the thrill of the upswings.

Another thing to note is that this is heavily predicated on the notion that you want to get to an in-person date ASAP. I personally find texting through these online services a complete waste of time and a terrible predictor of love interest. I can't tell you how many times someone seemed like a great match until I met them. The best thing, in my opinion, is to figure out how to get your would-be partner with you in a café having expended the least time and energy possible and see if the sparks fly once the two of you are there.

Lastly, I want to touch on one thing that is well covered in the guides, but I don't think is emphasized nearly enough. Dating is a skill, like any other. You know how you get good at dating? By dating. A lot. There's no other solution. You can read up all you want, but eventually you NEED to practice. Do you think anyone can learn to play guitar just by reading a bunch on how to do it and trying it once? No! The idea is ridiculous. Dating is no different.

If you get serious about this, you are going to spend many, many hours in awkward and uncomfortable situations with nothing to say on first dates. But that will harden you. It will make you stronger, and better. (Imagine "Eye of the Tiger" playing during your dating montage, if it helps. Or you could pick "No Easy Way Out." That is, of course, if you have no taste.)

One thing I did to help bootstrap when I was first getting started was that I adopted the "Starbucks rule." Back then, I went to Starbucks once a day. I waited in line for about two minutes to order and then waited a few more to get my drink. Each day, I would see new people. I made a rule that I had to talk to the stranger either in front of me or behind me every time I went, regardless of who or what they were.

At first this was awkward. I would turn around and say, "Hi!" Then the two of us would look at each other uncomfortably. Then I would turn back around and it would be SUPER WEIRD. Eventually I learned to say, "Hi, I'm Colin. How are you today?" and as I practiced more and more it became less creepy and more normal. Once it was a routine, I stopped even having to think about it. Doing this helped a lot with dating, as I could just imagine (and sometimes I didn't have to!) that they were the person behind me in line at Starbucks. On a tangential note, if you adopt the talking-to-strangers rule I recommend skipping people under eighteen. It's CREEPY when you try and talk to a six-year-old out of the blue at Starbucks. Don't be like me and learn that one the hard way.

Using these strategies, I someday hope to find a lady who thinks my analytical and systematic approach to life is sexy: one who wants to make sweet love to me under the soft glow of my pivot tables.

COLIN BUNDSCHU is a starving graduate student fighting his way through snow and physics in Ithaca, NY. Notoriously single, and less notoriously debonair, he fears only two things: knives and escalators. He's also a connoisseur of fine handshakes, so be sure to lotion up before meeting him.

But let's get real for a second. Who is Colin Bundschu? The truth is, no one really knows. Some say that he crawled from the mouth of a volcano, spewed from Earth's fiery core like a human hairball. Others suggest that unhinged scientists created him in a deranged experiment to create a delicious hybrid between Taco Bell and Mountain Dew. And yet some still contend that he arrived one day in the mail, a mis-delivered infomercial product with no return label. Whatever his origins, he's very handsome. And single. Did we mention that last part? Just saying ...

CPSIA information can be obtained
at www.ICGtesting.com
Printed in the USA
FFOW02n1323260417
35024FF